New wave

English
in practice

Daily practice workbook

Name:

www.prim-ed.com

New wave English in practice *(6th Class)*

Published by Prim-Ed Publishing® 2014
Copyright© R.I.C. Publications® 2014
ISBN 978-1-84654-733-1
6225IRE

Titles available in this series:
New wave English in practice *(1st Class)*
New wave English in practice *(2nd Class)*
New wave English in practice *(3rd Class)*
New wave English in practice *(4th Class)*
New wave English in practice *(5th Class)*
New wave English in practice *(6th Class)*
New wave English in practice teachers guide for classes 1–6

SAY
NO
TO
BULLYING!

NOBODY DESERVES TO BE BULLIED.
TELL AN ADULT YOU CAN TRUST.

This anti-bullying campaign is supported by the Irish Educational Publishers' Association.

Prim-Ed Publishing
Marshmeadows
New Ross
Co. Wexford
Ireland
email: sales@prim-ed.com
web: www.prim-ed.com

FOREWORD

In this daily practice workbook you will be able to develop your ability to use English. Each day, you will have questions to answer in the areas of spelling, word study, punctuation and grammar. The 150 days of questions are broken into 15 units of 10 days. Each unit has a focus, which will help to improve your English skills as well as your knowledge about how language works.

At the completion of each set of 10 days, you will have the opportunity to test what you learnt by doing some revision questions.

Your daily scores are recorded in the bubble at the bottom of each day. These daily scores can be transferred onto the pupil record sheets at the front of your book. This will give an overview of your performance for the whole school year.

Be sure to read each question carefully before you answer it. If you find a question too difficult, move on to the next one. If you have time at the end you can go back to the one you haven't done.

CONTENTS

Pupil record sheet

Unit 1

Date			
Day 1		Day 6	
Day 2		Day 7	
Day 3		Day 8	
Day 4		Day 9	
Day 5		Day 10	
Revision			

Unit 2

Date			
Day 11		Day 16	
Day 12		Day 17	
Day 13		Day 18	
Day 14		Day 19	
Day 15		Day 20	
Revision			

Unit 3

Date			
Day 21		Day 26	
Day 22		Day 27	
Day 23		Day 28	
Day 24		Day 29	
Day 25		Day 30	
Revision			

Unit 4

Date			
Day 31		Day 36	
Day 32		Day 37	
Day 33		Day 38	
Day 34		Day 39	
Day 35		Day 40	
Revision			

Unit 5

Date			
Day 41		Day 46	
Day 42		Day 47	
Day 43		Day 48	
Day 44		Day 49	
Day 45		Day 50	
Revision			

Unit 6

Date			
Day 51		Day 56	
Day 52		Day 57	
Day 53		Day 58	
Day 54		Day 59	
Day 55		Day 60	
Revision			

Unit 7

Date			
Day 61		Day 66	
Day 62		Day 67	
Day 63		Day 68	
Day 64		Day 69	
Day 65		Day 70	
Revision			

Unit 8

Date			
Day 71		Day 76	
Day 72		Day 77	
Day 73		Day 78	
Day 74		Day 79	
Day 75		Day 80	
Revision			

Pupil record sheet

Unit 9

Date		
Day 81		Day 86
Day 82		Day 87
Day 83		Day 88
Day 84		Day 89
Day 85		Day 90
Revision		

Unit 10

Date		
Day 91		Day 96
Day 92		Day 97
Day 93		Day 98
Day 94		Day 99
Day 95		Day 100
Revision		

Unit 11

Date		
Day 101		Day 106
Day 102		Day 107
Day 103		Day 108
Day 104		Day 109
Day 105		Day 110
Revision		

Unit 12

Date		
Day 111		Day 116
Day 112		Day 117
Day 113		Day 118
Day 114		Day 119
Day 115		Day 120
Revision		

Unit 13

Date		
Day 121		Day 126
Day 122		Day 127
Day 123		Day 128
Day 124		Day 129
Day 125		Day 130
Revision		

Unit 14

Date		
Day 131		Day 136
Day 132		Day 137
Day 133		Day 138
Day 134		Day 139
Day 135		Day 140
Revision		

Unit 15

Date		
Day 141		Day 146
Day 142		Day 147
Day 143		Day 148
Day 144		Day 149
Day 145		Day 150
Revision		

DAY 1

1. Correct the spelling mistake. _____

   How long is a lenth of string?

2. Circle the correct spelling.   suprise   surprise

3. Which word is spelt incorrectly?   braek   brake

4. In *histry*, the missing vowel is ⬚ .

5. A synonym for *brief* is _____ .

   soon   short   near

6. Add the prefix *auto* to one word to make a new word.

   marine   biography   _____

7. Write as a contraction.

   has not _____

8. Write the homophone of *hole*. _____

9. Separate *friendship* into its syllables.

   _____

10. Write the plural of *library*. _____

11. Complete the punctuation.

    my favourite fruits are apples and bananas

12. Circle the words that should have capital letters.

    australia   beijing   japanese   countries

13. Write **!** or **?**

    'Hurry, we need to catch this bus ⬚ *'*

14. How many nouns? ⬚

    Jill and her mother came on a plane from London.

15. Circle and write the proper noun. _____

    Jill loves to perform for an audience.

16. Circle the two common nouns.

    At the concert, Jill sang three songs.

17. Circle the two adjectives.

    The big city is a new experience for Jill.

18. Circle the proper adjectives.

    Jill loves to play Italian, Greek and Irish music.

19. Circle the pronoun and the nouns it refers to.

    Jill and her mother enjoy walking in the parks where they meet lots of people.

20. Circle the pronoun and the noun it refers to.

    As soon as the phone rang, it was answered.

DAY 2

1. Correct the spelling mistake. _____

   There are vairious ways to stay fit and healthy.

2. Circle the incorrect spelling.   probably   probly

3. Which word is spelt incorrectly?   noes   knows

4. Rearrange the letters to make the word that means *badly behaved*.

   aghntuy   _____

5. An antonym for *predator* is _____ .

   hunter   prefect   prey

6. Add the suffix *less* to one word to make a new word.

   age   soft   _____

7. Write *breath* and *breathe* in the correct places.

   When I am short of _____ *, I try to*

   _____ *deeply.*

8. Write a synonym for *courage*.   b_____

9. In the dictionary, ... comes before *immediate*.

   ⬚ important   ⬚ impatient   ⬚ imagine

10. Circle the word which does not have the *ew* (new) sound.

    broom   crew   door   humour

11. Complete the punctuation.

    Tom asked Please may I be excused?

12. Add commas to the sentence.

    You can see lions bears otters and zebras at the zoo.

13. Write **!** or **?**

    'Which way shall we go ⬚ *'*

14. Circle and write the verbs.   _____   _____

    Kim began a new school and has new friends.

15. Circle and write the verb group. _____

    Kim has been swimming with her friends.

16. Circle and write the verb group. _____

    Tomorrow, Kim will be dancing in a competition.

17. Circle and write the verb. _____

    Yesterday, Kim played netball in a tournament.

18. Circle and write the adverb. _____

    Mark played the violin beautifully.

19. Circle and write the adverb. _____

    Kim and Mark have settled quickly into their new school.

20. Circle the preposition.

    Kim and Mark's house is behind the park.

MY SCORE

MY SCORE

DAY 3

1. Correct the spelling mistake. _____

   Not every question has a simple arnser.

2. Circle the correct spelling.   interest   intrest

3. Which word is spelt incorrectly?   bouy   boy

4. Circle the correct spelling.   natchural   natural

5. A synonym for **hasty** is _____ .

   delicious   fast   impatient

6. Add the prefix **dis** to one word to make a new word.

   polite   honest   _____

7. The contraction **must've** is made from the words

   _____ and _____ .

8. **Weight** is a homophone of _____ .

9. Separate **arrival** into its syllables.

   _____

10. The plural of **monkey** is _____ .

11. Complete the punctuation.

    the ship visited ports in italy, france and spain.

12. Add speech marks to the sentence.

    Amir cried, I do love travelling to different countries!

13. Add **!** or **?**

    'Which cities are near the coast ☐ *'*

14. How many nouns? ☐

    Alice felt her face go red with embarrassment.

15. Circle and write the abstract noun. _____

    She had a great fear of the big waves.

16. Circle and write the two nouns. _____ _____

    Everyone except Alice was enjoying the water.

17. Circle the two adjectives.

    As a young girl, Alice loved to play in the salty water.

18. Circle the comparative adjective.

    But one day, the sea was rougher than usual.

19. Circle the pronoun and the noun it refers to.

    A huge wave knocked Alice over and it dragged Alice back into the water.

20. Circle the noun that the pronoun **she** refers to.

    Sue helped Alice as she tried to stand up.

DAY 4

1. Circle the correct spelling.   early   urly

2. Circle the correct spelling.   offen   often

3. Which word is spelt incorrectly?   doe   duogh

4. Circle the correct spelling.   among   amung

5. An antonym for **certain** is _____ .

   definite   doubtful   probable

6. Add the suffix **ness** to one word to make a new word.

   care   weak   _____

7. Write **allowed** and **aloud** in the correct places.

   I am _____ to sing _____ , but only in the shower.

8. The part of the words that means **sound** is _____ .

   microphone   symphony   telephone

9. In the dictionary, ... comes after **occasion**.

   ☐ ocean   ☐ obvious   ☐ obtain

10. Which word does not have the **ou** (out) sound?

    ☐ doubt   ☐ mouse   ☐ thought   ☐ plough

11. Add an apostrophe.

    The babies nappies needed changing.

12. Which is correct?   ☐ children's toys
                            ☐ childrens' toys

13. Add a comma to the sentence.

    A nutritious inexpensive children's menu was available.

14. Circle and write the verbs. _____ _____

    Ben and Amy help their dad who builds bicycles.

15. Circle and write the verb group. _____

    Their dad has been building bikes for over 30 years.

16. Circle and write the verb group. _____

    Now, Ben and Amy can repair their own bikes.

17. Circle and write the adjectives. _____

    The ambitious twins would love to run a successful shop in the future.

18. Circle and write the adverb. _____

    They have organised their bike shed thoughtfully.

19. Circle and write the adverb. _____

    The twins work carefully with the bike tools.

20. Circle the preposition.

    They spend all their spare time in the bike shed.

MY SCORE

MY SCORE

DAY 5

1. Correct the spelling mistake. _____
   Cough medersin sometimes tastes like strawberries.

2. Circle the correct spelling.   experiense   experience

3. Which word is spelt incorrectly?   threw   thruogh

4. Circle the correct spelling.   escape   excape

5. A synonym for **clear** is _____.
   clean   shiny   transparent

6. Add the prefix **anti** to one word to make a new word.
   social   energy   _____

7. Write as a contraction.
   might not   _____

8. Write the homophone of **flower**. _____

9. Separate **calculator** into its syllables.
   _____

10. Write the plural of **address**. _____

11. Complete the punctuation.
    What a beautiful bouquet exclaimed Sinéad.

12. Add commas to the sentence.
    Tom said 'Yesterday I ran swam and played tennis.'

13. Add an apostrophe.
    James and Ians parents were Don and Susan.

14. How many nouns? ☐
    Ryan did his homework then played on his computer.

15. Is the word **wanted** a verb?   ☐ yes ☐ no
    His mum wanted him to help with the housework.

16. Circle the proper noun.
    Ryan left his clothes, books and games on the floor.

17. The adjective compares:
    ☐ two things   ☐ more than two things
    Ryan is the worst of his brothers for making a mess.

18. The adjective compares:
    ☐ two things   ☐ more than two things
    Even Ryan's 5-year-old brother is better than he is.

19. Circle the pronoun and the noun it refers to.
    Dad says that although he is messy, Ryan is not lazy.

20. Circle the pronoun and the noun it refers to.
    Ryan works in the garden, planting vegetables and harvesting them for Mum to cook.

DAY 6

1. Correct the spelling mistake. _____
   The magician can make you dissappear in a flash.

2. Circle the correct spelling.   occassion   occasion

3. Which word is spelt incorrectly?   riegn   rain

4. Circle the correct spelling.   truely   truly

5. An antonym for **curious** is _____.
   strange   uninterested   wondrous

6. Add the suffix **ful** to one word to make a new word.
   enjoy   harm   _____

7. Write **bought** and **brought** in the correct places.
   She _____ a gift and _____ it to the party.

8. The part of the words that means **far off** is _____.
   television   telephone   telegraph

9. In the dictionary, ... comes after **height**.
   ☐ heard   ☐ heart   ☐ history

10. Which word does not have the **long a** (make) sound?
    ☐ major ☐ occasion ☐ natural ☐ daily

11. Complete the punctuation.
    What's on TV tonight asked Samir.

12. Add a comma to the question.
    Are sport music and films included in the quiz?

13. Add an apostrophe.
    Jims comic collection

14. Circle the infinitive of the underlined verb.
    to be   to have   to go
    The Eiffel Tower is a famous landmark in Paris, France.

15. Circle and write the verb group. _____
    The Eiffel Tower was completed in 1889.

16. Circle and write the verb group. _____
    You can walk the 600 steps to the second level.

17. The verb is in the: ☐ past tense ☐ present tense
    Most visitors ride in the lifts to the three viewing platforms.

18. Circle and write the adverb. _____
    The Eiffel Tower rises majestically above the city.

19. Circle and write the adverb. _____
    Stairs to the third level are usually closed to the public.

20. Circle the proper noun.
    Visitors to the Eiffel Tower may have to wait for a few hours in a long queue.

MY SCORE

DAY 7

1. Correct the spelling mistake. _____

   Febuary is the second month of the year.

2. Circle the correct spelling.   quarter   quater

3. Which word is spelt incorrectly?   vien   vane

4. Circle the correct spelling.   mystry   mystery

5. A synonym for **abandon** is _____ .

   destroy   desert   support

6. Add the prefix **mis** to one word to make a new word.

   able   fire   _____

7. The contraction **they're** is made from the words

   _____ and _____ .

8. Write the homophone of **pain**.   _____

9. Separate **removal** into its syllables.

   _____

10. The plural of **loaf** is _____ .

11. Circle the words that need capital letters.

    at the north pole, january days are cold and dark.

12. Add **!** or **?**

    'Have you seen the northern lights ☐' asked Adam.

13. Add **!** or **?**

    'There they are ☐' cried Cara.

14. Fill in the missing word.

    A group of birds is sometimes called a _____.

15. Circle the collective nouns.

    A pack of dogs was chasing a herd of cattle.

16. Circle the collective nouns.

    A colony of penguins was attacked by a pod of seals.

17. Which is correct?   ☐ larger   ☐ more large

    Adult Emperor penguins are .... than adult Adelie penguins.

18. Which is correct?   ☐ ferociousest
                          ☐ most ferocious

    Leopard seals are one of the .... marine predators.

19. Circle the pronoun and the noun it refers to.

    Female leopard seals are bigger than the males. They can weigh up to 600 kg.

20. Circle the pronoun and the nouns it refers to.

    Natural predators of seals are killer whales and great white sharks, but they are not their greatest threat.

DAY 8

1. Correct the spelling mistake. _____

   The wizard started his life as an ordinry boy.

2. Circle the correct spelling.   beleive   believe

3. Which word is spelt incorrectly?   peice   peace

4. Circle the correct spelling.   plastick   plastic

5. An antonym for **accept** is _____ .

   except   reject   receive

6. Add the suffix **able** to one word to make a new word.

   suit   waste   _____

7. Write **allowed** or **aloud** in the sentence.

   The children are not _____ to leave the school premises.

8. Write a synonym for **ancient**.   o_____

9. In the dictionary, ... comes after **thought**.

   ☐ therefore   ☐ through   ☐ though

10. Which word does not have the **oa** (boat) sound?

    ☐ elbow   ☐ oboe   ☐ bough   ☐ smoke

11. Add an apostrophe to show possession.

    Mondays practice is the last one of the term.

12. Circle the correctly punctuated phrase.

    the teams' effort   the team's effort

13. Add a comma or commas to the sentence.

    The enthusiastic dedicated team was well rewarded.

14. Which pronoun matches the verb?

    ☐ I   ☐ you   ☐ it   ☐ we   ☐ they

    Mount Everest <u>is</u> the world's highest mountain.

15. Circle the verb group.

    Many people would like to climb Mount Everest.

16. Circle and write the verb group. _____

    Many people have died on this mountain.

17. The verb is in the: ☐ past tense ☐ present tense

    People are still climbing Mount Everest.

18. Circle and write the adverb. _____

    Climbers prepare carefully for such a climb.

19. Circle and write the adverb. _____

    Families hope that climbers return safely.

20. Circle the conjunction.

    Since the summit was first reached over 60 years ago, many people have climbed Mount Everest.

MY SCORE

MY SCORE

DAY 9

1. Correct the spelling mistake. _____
   The gide showed us around the medieval castle.

2. Circle the correct spelling. userly usually

3. Which word is spelt incorrectly? horse haorse

4. Circle the correct spelling. voyage voyaje

5. A synonym for **caught** is _____ .
   entangled released hidden

6. Add the prefix **im** to one word to make a new word.
   possible responsible _____

7. Write as a contraction.
   does not _____

8. Write the homophone of **heir**. _____

9. Separate **ability** into its syllables.
   _____

10. Write the plural of **calf**. _____

11. Complete the punctuation.
    At the end of the day the sun slipped out of sight

12. Add speech marks to show what was said.
    I can't believe you just did that! cried Ava.

13. Add an apostrophe to show possession.
    The cats tails swayed in unison.

14. How many nouns? ☐
    The name of a young swan is a cygnet.

15. Circle the masculine noun.
    A male swan is a cob and a female is a pen.

16. Circle and write the collective noun. _____
    There can be up to eight eggs in each clutch.

17. Which is correct? ☐ bigger ☐ more big
    Cobs are usually .... than pens.

18. Which is correct? ☐ protectiver
    ☐ more protective
    Swans are .... of their young than some birds.

19. Circle the pronoun and the noun it refers to.
    Mute swans are quieter than other species but they make a lot of noise with their wings.

20. Circle the pronoun and the noun it refers to.
    When they migrate, swans fly in a v-shaped formation called a wedge.

DAY 10

1. Correct the spelling mistake. _____
   I change my books at the libery every week.

2. Circle the correct spelling. doesn't dosen't

3. Which word is spelt incorrectly? caorse course

4. Circle the correct spelling. urgent urggent

5. An antonym for **regular** is _____ .
   uniform random always

6. Add the suffix **ation** to one word to make a new word.
   inform reverse _____

7. Write **break** and **brake** in the correct places.
   The _____ on the cart could _____ if pulled too hard.

8. Write a synonym for **halt**. s_____

9. In the dictionary, ... comes after **devour**.
   ☐ devious ☐ devote ☐ devout

10. Which word does not have the **ew** (new) sound?
    ☐ queue ☐ beauty ☐ hood ☐ feud

11. Complete the punctuation.
    If you go to the library can I come too asked Ian

12. Add commas to the statement.
    I have visited Thailand Vietnam France and Spain.

13. Add an apostrophe.
    My parents travel plans

14. The pronoun matches the verb:
    ☐ I ☐ you ☐ it ☐ we ☐ they
    World travel is the dream of many people.

15. Circle and write the verb group. _____
    The novel Around the world in 80 days was written by the French writer, Jules Verne.

16. Circle and write the verb. _____
    The book describes a journey across the globe.

17. The verb is in the: ☐ past tense ☐ present tense
    Phileas Fogg is challenged to travel around the world in 80 days.

18. Circle and write the adverb. _____
    Fogg accepts the challenge eagerly.

19. Circle and write the adverb. _____
    Fogg and his servant, Passepartout, leave immediately.

20. Circle the pronoun.
    Eighty days later, Fogg's challengers wait with great hope that he will not succeed.

MY SCORE

MY SCORE

DAY 11

1. Correct the spelling mistake. _____

   That new paint colour makes a diferance.

2. Circle the correct spelling.   veyicle   vehicle

3. Rearrange the letters to spell the word that means *well-known*.

   smafuo   _____

4. Circle the correct spelling.   perticular   particular

5. *Often* is a synonym for _____ .

   frequently   sometimes   never

6. Add a prefix to give each word the opposite meaning.

   _____active   _____regular

7. Write as a contraction.

   should have   _____

8. Write the homophone of *mussel*. _____

9. Separate *persuade* into its syllables. _____

10. The plural of *curiosity* is _____ .

11. Add speech marks to show what was said.

    What a fantastic view! marvelled Dad.

12. Add commas to the sentence.

    'I can see our house the library the hospital and the school!' cried Michelle excitedly.

13. Add capital letters where necessary.

    i live at 52 highgate terrace in the town of sligo.

14. The underlined words are adjectives. ⬜ yes   ⬜ no

    The climb to the top of the mountain was tough.

15. Write the abstract noun. _____

    Jim's progress was slow but his legs kept moving.

16. Circle the verbs.

    He ate his lunch as he gazed at the beautiful view.

17. Circle the abstract noun.

    As he walked down the mountain, Jim was filled with pride.

18. Circle the noun that the pronoun refers to.

    The walk had been long, but Jim had enjoyed it.

19. Circle the noun that the pronoun refers to.

    Jim took off his boots and cleaned their soles with a brush before putting them in the car.

20. Circle the pronoun and the nouns it refers to.

    Jim and his father shared thoughts about the day and agreed the day had been very good for them.

MY SCORE

DAY 12

1. Correct the spelling mistake. _____

   I took the next avalable appointment at the dentist.

2. Circle the correct spelling.   yacht   yatch

3. Rearrange the letters to spell the word that means *wonderful*.

   aellmorsuv   _____

4. Circle the correct spelling.   eighth   eightt

5. *Miraculous* is an antonym for _____ .

   fortunate   disastrous   shameful

6. Write the word made when the suffix *ness* is added.

   happy   _____   sad   _____

7. Write *rhyme* and *rhythm* in the correct places.

   Put to music, the _____ had a good

   _____ .

8. The prefix *semi* (*semicircle*) means _____ .

9. In the dictionary, ... comes after *avenue*.

   ⬜ available   ⬜ avalanche   ⬜ average

10. Choose to complete the words.   ere   are   ear

    Prep_____ the p_____ over th_____ .

11. Complete the punctuation.

    That boys results were excellent.

12. Add an apostrophe.

    Many neighbours children were at the meeting.

13. Add a comma.

    Since it is dark I will stay inside.

14. Write the verb group. _____

    These days, we can travel by many forms of transport.

15. Which tense?   ⬜ past   ⬜ present

    We travel on foot or by bike to keep healthy.

16. Insert the verb.   travels   travel

    He would _____ by bike every day if he could.

17. Insert the verb.   take   takes

    The bus ride may _____ about 20 minutes.

18. Write the pronoun.

    _____ might read her book on the train.

19. Write the pronoun.

    If necessary, _____ will take his car.

20. Write the pronoun.

    If _____ can fly to the city, her journey will take much less time.

MY SCORE

DAY 13

1. Correct the spelling mistake. _____

    I got a briuse when I walked into the open door.

2. Circle the correct spelling.   system   sistem

3. Rearrange the letters to spell the word that means **extremely old**.

    aceinnt   _____

4. Circle the correct spelling.   hite   height

5. A synonym for **enough** is _____ .

    excessive   sufficient   inadequate

6. Add the prefix that means **again**.

    _____appear   _____live

7. The contraction **they'll** is made from the words

    _____ and _____ .

8. Write the homophone of **groan**. _____

9. Separate **frequently** into its syllables.

    _____

10. The plural of **potato** is _____ .

11. Insert a suitable word.

    In the mornings, my brother is never _____ for school on time.

12. Add commas.

    My favourite subjects are English Irish geography and history.

13. Add a comma.

    Although I like maths I find problem solving difficult.

14. Circle the definite articles.

    At the beach, we saw a dolphin close to the shore.

15. Circle any indefinite articles.

    A man in a kayak was very close to the dolphin.

16. Write the definite article. _____

    The man was really pleased to have seen such a beautiful creature.

17. Circle the preposition.

    We kept looking at the ocean but the dolphin had gone.

18. Write the preposition. _____

    We knelt on the sand and dug a huge hole.

19. Circle the conjunction.

    We sat in the hole and waited for the water to rush in.

20. Write the conjunction. _____

    The water came in but it did not fill the hole.

MY SCORE

DAY 14

1. Correct the spelling mistake. _____

    The neighbour's barking dog is a newsance.

2. Circle the correct spelling.   simbal   symbol

3. Rearrange the letters to spell the word that means **brave**.

    racogue   _____

4. Circle the correct spelling.   seperate   separate

5. **Stressed** is an antonym for _____ .

    different   clumsy   relaxed

6. Write the new word made by adding the suffix **ous**.

    courage   _____

    outrage   _____

7. Write **stair** or **stare** in the sentence.

    Why does your dog always _____ at me?

8. Write an antonym for **singular**.   p_____

9. In the dictionary, ... comes after **convenience**.

    ☐ correct   ☐ community   ☐ conscious

10. Which letters complete the words?   tu or tch

    frac____re   pos____re   fea____re

11. Circle the mistake.

    I am flying to europe to visit my aunt Ella.

12. Add commas.

    While there I will visit Italy Austria Germany and Hungary.

13. Circle the verb group.

    My aunt will meet me in Vienna.

14. Circle the adjective.

    Aunt Ella lives in the beautiful city of Vienna.

15. Write the adjective. _____

    Marie Antoinette, the famous queen of France, was born in Vienna.

16. Circle the proper adjective.

    Vienna is the Austrian capital city.

17. Write the proper adjective. _____

    I will visit Vienna while on a European river cruise.

18. Circle the adverb.

    Marie Antoinette stood proudly before her execution.

19. Write the adverb. _____

    The guillotine fell quickly and the queen was dead.

20. Circle the verbs.

    The crowd cheered loudly and celebrated wildly.

MY SCORE

DAY 15

1. Correct the spelling mistake. _____

   Travelling to foregn countries extends the mind.

2. Circle the correct spelling.   definite   definate

3. Correct the spelling mistake. _____

   The spy's idenntity was soon discovered.

4. Circle the correct spelling.   consious   conscious

5. A synonym for **relevant** is _____ .

   religious   related   reliable

6. Add a prefix to give each word the opposite meaning.

   _____agree   _____belief

7. Write as a contraction.

   they have   _____

8. Write the homophone of **board**. _____

9. Separate **existence** into its syllables.

   _____

10. The plural of **stomach** is _____ .

11. Add speech marks to show what was said.

    What career would you like to have? asked Mr Moore.

12. Add commas to the sentence.

    'An astronaut a firefighter a zookeeper or the president!' answered Kian excitedly.

13. Add capital letters where necessary.

    The planets in our solar system include earth, mars, mercury and venus.

14. Circle the concrete noun.

    The weather is very important to firefighters.

15. Write the abstract noun. _____

    To work in a zoo, you need an interest in animals.

16. Circle the better word.   anger   trust

    Can we put our .... in politicians?

17. Circle the abstract noun.

    There was peace in the room.

18. Circle the noun that the pronoun refers to.

    The spacecraft orbited the moon before landing on <u>it</u>.

19. Circle the noun that the pronoun refers to.

    The firefighters tackled the fire for hours before <u>they</u> were successful.

20. Circle the pronoun and the noun it refers to.

    Zoo workers love the animals in their care and would do anything for them.

MY SCORE

DAY 16

1. Correct the spelling mistake. _____

   To be successful, it is necessry to work hard.

2. Circle the correct spelling.   devellop   develop

3. Correct the spelling mistake. _____

   I want a career in the medical proffession.

4. Circle the correct spelling.   pressure   preshure

5. An antonym for **separate** is _____ .

   smooth   join   wrong

6. Add the suffix **ise** or **en** and write the verb.

   fright _____   terror _____

7. Write **loose** and **lose** in the correct places.

   If I _____ my button, my trousers will be

   _____ .

8. Write a synonym for **glance**.   I_____

9. In the dictionary, ... comes after **forecast**.

   ☐ foreign   ☐ force   ☐ forbid

10. Which word does not have the **soft g** sound?

    ☐ prejudice   ☐ privilege   ☐ suggest

    ☐ signature

11. Complete the punctuation.

    Where is the Andes mountain range asked Miss Walsh.

12. Add an apostrophe to show possession.

    Earths longest mountain range is under the ocean.

13. Add a comma.

    This term we shall study mountains.

14. Circle the verb group.

    We will climb mountains.

15. The main verb is _____ .

    We will climb up to 500 metres.

16. The pronoun is _____ .

    We will climb a different mountain each week.

17. Tick: ☐ **with**   ☐ **for**

    We climb that peak often and .... determination.

18. Tick: ☐ **in**   ☐ **on**

    The mountains .... the coast are tricky to climb.

19. Circle the word that is not needed.

    With this weather, we will be down at the summit very soon.

20. Tick the correct word: ☐ **they're**   ☐ **their**

    The climbers on the ridge are celebrating .... achievement.

MY SCORE

DAY 17

1. Correct the spelling mistake. _____
   I did not recernise you with your new haircut.

2. Circle the correct spelling.   dicsionary   dictionary

3. Correct the spelling mistake. _____
   Mum does not like that vareiety of apple.

4. Circle the correct spelling.   neighbour   nieghbour

5. A synonym for **reliable** is _____ .
   trusting   dependable   confident

6. Add the prefix to make a word that means **the reverse**.
   _____frost   _____value

7. The contraction **might've** is made from the words
   _____ and _____ .

8. Write the homophone of **meddle**. _____

9. Separate **develop** into its syllables. _____

10. The plural of **watch** is _____ .

11. Add commas.

   Rhythmic gymnastics unlike other forms of the sport requires the use of a ball a ribbon a hoop and clubs.

12. Circle the simile.

   My friend is as agile as a monkey when she performs gymnastics.

13. Circle the proper adjective.

   Last year, a Chinese gymnast won the competition.

14. Circle the verbs.

   I was amazed by my friend's skill as she performed the tricky routine.

15. Is the word **apparatus** used correctly? ☐ yes ☐ no

   In every routine, she caught all her apparatus.

16. Circle the mistake.

   This year, my friend has won a meddle at every event.

17. Circle the preposition.

   She threw the ball and it landed on her shoulders.

18. Write the preposition. _____

   She swirled the ribbon around her body.

19. Circle the conjunction.

   I would have stayed longer, but I had to leave.

20. Write the conjunction. _____

   My friend is very fit because she trains so hard.

DAY 18

1. Correct the spelling mistake. _____
   Do not interuppt when I am speaking!

2. Circle the correct spelling.   leisure   leosure

3. Correct the spelling mistake. _____
   I cannot perswade Mum to let me go to the party.

4. Circle the correct spelling.   soldier   souldier

5. An antonym for **interfere** is _____ .
   hinder   assist   fascinate

6. Write the noun made by adding the suffix **ion**.
   attract   _____
   conclude   _____

7. Write **accept** and **except** in the correct places.
   We _____ all donations _____ electrical goods.

8. Write an antonym for **honest**.   d_____

9. In the dictionary, ... comes after **inject**.
   ☐ inhale   ☐ inflate   ☐ innocent   ☐ initial

10. Add letters to complete the words.   gu   gue
    lea_____   _____itar   pla_____   _____ard

11. Add **?** or **!**.

    How do volcanoes form ☐

12. Add commas.
    Mount Etna on the island of Sicily is an active volcano.

13. Circle the word that is not needed.
    An active volcano is one that could erupt at any night time.

14. Write **taller** or **tallest**.
    In fact, Mount Etna is the _____ active volcano in Europe.

15. Circle the verb group.
    It has erupted many times in the past.

16. Circle the abstract noun.
    Tourists admire the beauty of the area.

17. Write the proper adjective. _____
    I am very interested in Italian culture.

18. Circle the proper noun.
    The town of Catania is located quite near the volcano.

19. The opposite of an active volcano is:
    ☐ dormer   ☐ dormant   ☐ dormitory

20. Is the meaning correct? ☐ yes ☐ no

    Authorities divert the volcano away from the surrounding towns and villages.

MY SCORE

MY SCORE

1. Correct the spelling mistake. _____
   My house is butween the school and the park.

2. Circle the correct spelling.   hospidal   hospital

3. Correct the spelling mistake. _____
   I am foretunate to live in a beautiful country.

4. Circle the correct spelling.   ready   reddy

5. A synonym for **doubt** is _____ .
   problem   question   certainty

6. Add the prefix that means **before**.
   _____history   _____view

7. Write as a contraction.
   you had   _____

8. Write the homophone of **peer**. _____

9. Separate **necessary** into its syllables. _____

10. The plural of **echo** is _____ .

11. Add the apostrophe.
    The twins grandmother gave them a special treat.

12. Add the apostrophe.
    One twins score was better than expected.

13. Tick: ☐ **is called**   ☐ **are called.**
    Jacob's and Isaac's dogs .... Archie and Roxy.

14. Write the correct part of the verb **to be**.
    Jacob and Isaac _____ Paul and Ann's only children.

15. Write the proper nouns. _____ _____
    Paul and Ann each have two siblings.

16. Common or proper nouns? _____
    Jacob and Isaac have two <u>aunts</u> and two <u>uncles</u>.

17. Choose the noun.   cousins   nieces   nephews
    The children of their aunts and uncles are the twins' _____ .

18. Tick: ☐ **enjoy**   ☐ **enjoys**
    The twins .... many special days with their family.

19. Write the verb. _____
    In her old-age, Ann hopes to be a grandmother.

20. Circle the indefinite articles.
    The twins have a new baby cousin, a new nephew for their dad.

1. Correct the spelling mistake. _____
   Exercise gives me more enurgy.

2. Circle the correct spelling.   damidge   damage

3. Correct the spelling mistake. _____
   I always keep a hankerchief in my pocket.

4. Circle the correct spelling.   dout   doubt

5. An antonym for **expand** is _____ .
   betrayal   belief   contract

6. Write the adjective made by adding the suffix **able**.
   adapt   _____
   agree   _____

7. Write **threw** and **through** in the correct places.
   I _____ the ball _____ the hoop.

8. Write a synonym for **cunning**.   s_____

9. In the dictionary, ... comes before **threat**.
   ☐ thrift   ☐ thread   ☐ thresh

10. Circle the word that does not have a silent consonant.
    ghost   king   lamb   autumn

11. Tick: ☐ **is**   ☐ **are**.
    The Bayeux Tapestry, a medieval comic strip of historic events, ... on display in the French town.

12. Circle the word that is not needed.
    The tiny tapestry, created after a famous battle in 1066, is almost 70 metres long.

13. Add two commas.
    The battle known as the Battle of Hastings was short.

14. The verb group is _____ .
    The English king was killed by an arrow to his eye.

15. Write the proper adjective. _____
    The English had been defeated.

16. Write the main verb. _____
    The Normans had won the battle.

17. The conjunction is _____ .
    The Normans had won, but England would rise again.

18. Circle the pronoun.
    England and France were often at war because they were both powerful nations.

19. The preposition is _____ .
    Peace between England and France did not last long.

20. Circle the preposition.
    Sovereigns rule over their subjects.

MY SCORE

MY SCORE

DAY 21

1. Correct the spelling mistake. _____

   John's spelling test results were disastrus.

2. Circle the correct spelling.   peculiar   perculiar

3. Correct the spelling mistake. _____

   John did not menshun his test results to his parents.

4. Circle the correct spelling.   certin   certain

5. A synonym for **delete** is _____ .

   erase   cheat   hinder

6. Add the same prefix to make the opposites.

   _____order   _____connect

7. Write as a contraction.

   will not   _____

8. Write the correct homophone. _____

   The strong gust of wind blew/blue out the candle.

9. Separate **different** into its syllables. _____

10. The singular of **loaves** is _____ .

11. Add a comma to give the sentence sense.

    'Come on, let's eat Mum. I'm starving!' said Bea.

12. Add a comma.

    Before eating you should always wash your hands.

13. Add commas to the list.

    To make pasta, you need flour eggs oil and salt.

14. Write the common noun. _____

    Our holiday begins on Friday.

15. Write the proper noun. _____

    Our holiday begins on Friday.

16. Circle the verb.

    Our holiday to the pyramids of Egypt starts on Friday.

17. Write the comparative adjective. _____

    A holiday away is better than staying at home.

18. Write the superlative adjective. _____

    Our best holiday so far has been to Cambodia.

19. Circle the adjective.

    We have gone on four holidays with the family.

20. Write the pronouns. _____

    The choice of where to go on holidays is mine, not yours!

DAY 22

1. Correct the spelling mistake. _____

   I think my favrite season is spring, or maybe autumn.

2. Circle the correct spelling.   populer   popular

3. Correct the spelling mistake. _____

   I just cannot diside which season is the best.

4. Circle the correct spelling.   serpose   suppose

5. An antonym for **admit** is:

   ☐ despise   ☐ deny   ☐ dislike

6. Write the new noun when the suffix **age** is added to:

   break   _____

   bag   _____

7. Write **prove** and **proof** in the correct places.

   Is there any _____ to _____ that I am guilty?

8. Write a synonym for **remedy**.   c_____

9. In the dictionary, ... comes before **decline**.

   ☐ decrease   ☐ decision   ☐ decorate

10. In which word is there a silent letter?

    knuckle   different   admit

11. Add an apostrophe.

    Dads job keeps him away from home quite a lot.

12. Add an apostrophe.

    My sisters bedrooms are untidier than mine.

13. Add an apostrophe.

    'My childrens rooms are a mess!' exclaimed Mum.

14. Circle the simile.

    My room is as neat as a pin.

15. Tick: ☐ command   ☐ question   ☐ statement

    I can change the washer in a tap.

16. Write the verb group. _____

    I will paint the walls of my room during the next holidays.

17. Circle the adverb.

    I prepared a shelf carefully before painting it.

18. A better word for **said** _____ .

    'You did a great job,' said Dad.

19. Circle the preposition.

    I would like to renovate an old house near the country.

20. Write the conjunction. _____

    Because I am so handy, Dad has fewer jobs to do.

DAY 23

1. Correct the spelling mistake. _____

   I was given a speshial gift on my birthday.

2. Circle the correct spelling.   acheive   achieve

3. Correct the spelling mistake. _____

   My acshual birthday was on Sunday but the party was on Saturday.

4. Circle the correct spelling.   forty   fourty

5. A synonym for **excellent** is:

   ☐ marvellous ☐ adequate ☐ reasonable

6. Choose the prefix **anti** or **ante**.

   _____freeze

7. Write as a contraction.

   shall not _____

8. Write the correct homophone. _____

   I need to <u>altar/alter</u> my jacket before I can wear it.

9. Separate **desperate** into its syllables.

   _____

10. The singular of **diaries** is _____ .

11. Add a comma to give the sentence sense.

    We do not unlike animals in the wild, hunt and kill prey.

12. Add one comma.

    After the first snowfall everywhere seemed silent.

13. Add commas to the list.

    In the snow, we play snowball fights build a snowman sledge down the hill and make snow angels.

14. Write the abstract noun. _____

    People have pleasure in playing in the snow.

15. A better verb for **said**. _____

    'Let me build a snowman!' <u>said</u> the child.

16. Tick: ☐ command ☐ question ☐ statement

    The huge snowman is melting.

17. Write the comparative adjective. _____

    I felt ill yesterday and today, I feel worse.

18. Write the superlative adjective. _____

    Being ill is the worst luck as I can't play in the snow.

19. Circle the plural nouns.

    My cousins came to build snowmen in our garden.

20. A better word for **lovely**. _____

    The <u>lovely</u> snowman started to melt.

DAY 24

1. Correct the spelling mistake. _____

   The school secertary is leaving this week.

2. Circle the correct spelling.   sacrifice   sacrafice

3. Correct the spelling mistake. _____

   My brother now has a regliar job during the holidays.

4. Circle the correct spelling.   desperate   desprate

5. An antonym for **different** is:

   ☐ regular ☐ usual ☐ similar

6. Write the adjective when the suffix **ous** is added to:

   adventure _____

   glory _____

7. Write **passed** and **past** in the correct places.

   I _____ the cinema at half

   _____ seven.

8. Write an antonym for **innocent**.   g_____

9. In the dictionary, **preview** comes before _____ .

   prevent   previous   pretend

10. Which word has the same middle sound as **caught**?

    ☐ though   ☐ thousand   ☐ thorough
    ☐ thought   ☐ through

11. Add apostrophes where necessary.

    Ronans party was held in the park, close to his grandparents house.

12. Add an apostrophe.

    Ronan cleaned his pet mices cage before his party.

13. Add an apostrophe.

    The geeses shed is shut at night to keep the fox out.

14. Tick: ☐ command ☐ question ☐ statement

    Could penguins fly if they had longer wings?

15. A better word for **said**. _____

    The scientist <u>said</u> he wasn't sure of the answer.

16. Circle the verb group.

    I would be interested in these theories.

17. Circle the adverb.

    Penguins cannot fly but they can swim superbly.

18. Complete the collective noun.

    a _____ of wolves

19. Circle the preposition.

    Penguin parents take turns with their precious egg.

20. Write the conjunction. _____

    A penguin chick is very vulnerable when it is first born.

MY SCORE

MY SCORE

DAY 25

1. Correct the spelling mistake. _____

    There are many diffrent species of birds.

2. Circle the correct spelling.   gard   guard

3. Correct the spelling mistake. _____

    Pictures can be attatcht to emails.

4. Circle the correct spelling.   occur   ocurr

5. A synonym for **variety** is:

    ☐ mixture   ☐ different   ☐ many

6. Write the prefix **il** or **in** to give the opposite meaning.

    _____appropriate   _____legal

7. Write as a contraction.

    you will   _____

8. Write the correct homophone. _____

    The polar <u>bare/bear</u> strode across the ice.

9. Separate **occupy** into its syllables. _____

10. The plural of **sheep** is _____ .

11. Add a comma to give the sentence sense.

    While Mum was cooking the dog ran away.

12. Add a comma.

    After a warm-up you should stretch before exercising.

13. Add commas to the list.

    Stretch the muscles in your legs arms neck back and shoulders.

14. Write the proper noun. _____

    There is a new continent in the Pacific Ocean.

15. Circle the verb.

    This vast, plastic rubbish patch is the size of Australia.

16. Tick: ☐ reduce   ☐ increase

    What can the world's nations do to .... this problem?

17. Write the comparative adjective. _____

    The plastic refuse problem is more severe than most people realise.

18. Write the superlative adjective. _____

    The problem is most severe in countries that do not have recycling centres.

19. Circle the pronoun.

    We should recycle as much as possible.

20. Write the conjunction. _____

    The problem is ours, so we must try to solve it.

DAY 26

1. Correct the spelling mistake. _____

    The Arctic and Antarctica are at oppersit poles.

2. Circle the correct spelling.   straight   strate

3. Correct the spelling mistake. _____

    I sergest we try to solve this problem calmly.

4. Circle the correct spelling.   awkward   orkword

5. An antonym for **contract** is:

    ☐ try   ☐ expand   ☐ many

6. Write the new noun when the suffix **ist** is added to:

    piano   _____

    archaeology   _____

7. Write **expand** or **contract**.

    If things stretch and enlarge, we say they

    _____ .

8. Write a synonym for **foe**.   e_____

9. In the dictionary, ... comes after **mallet**.

    ☐ malaria   ☐ mammoth   ☐ malice

10. In which word is **k** the silent letter?

    ☐ knowledge   ☐ duck   ☐ khaki

11. Write **it's** or **its**.

    An athlete's life is enjoyable but has _____problems.

12. Add an apostrophe.

    His five teammates support helped the athlete to victory.

13. Add an apostrophe.

    His teams belief in him was rewarded.

14. Tick: ☐ command   ☐ question   ☐ statement

    May I ride my bike to school today?

15. Circle the pronouns.

    You may ride your bike, but it might rain.

16. Write the collective word.

    A _____ of bees.

17. Circle the adverb that tells us **when**.

    I might try tomorrow as the weather should be better.

18. Circle the adverb that tells us **when**.

    We have met them before.

19. Circle the preposition.

    I can ride on the road but I must stay on the path.

20. Write the conjunction. _____

    Cycling can be dangerous when the roads are busy.

MY SCORE

MY SCORE

UNIT 3

DAY 27

1. Correct the spelling mistake. _____

   It is important to have enuff exercise.

2. Circle the correct spelling.   avridge   average

3. Correct the spelling mistake. _____

   My most rescent holiday was to Canada.

4. Circle the correct spelling.   bargain   barrgin

5. A synonym for **possibly** is:

   ☐ maybe   ☐ definitely   ☐ never

6. Choose the prefix **pro** or **pre**, meaning **before**.

   _____pay   _____view

7. Write as a contraction.

   do not   _____

8. Write the correct homophone. _____

   The heard/herd of zebra reached the lake.

9. Separate **imagine** into its syllables. _____

10. The singular of **rubbish** is _____ .

11. Add a comma to give the sentence sense.

    Before Dad could eat the cat jumped on to the table.

12. Add a comma.

    If a bus or train is full always offer your seat to an older person.

13. Add a comma or commas to the list.

    Public transport includes the bus the train and the ferry.

14. Write the plural nouns. _____ _____

    Children understand IT better than older people.

15. Write the word that is not needed. _____

    The patient people had been waiting outside for the shop to open soon.

16. Tick: ☐ command   ☐ question   ☐ statement

    The new version mobile phone is now available.

17. Circle the comparative adjectives.

    The new phone is dearer than the older model.

18. Write the superlative adjective. _____

    Of all the phone brands, mine is the cheapest.

19. Circle the nouns.

    My phone is so heavy, holding it to my head hurts my arm.

20. A better verb for **said**. _____

    Dad said I could use his as it's better than mine.

DAY 28

1. Correct the spelling mistake. _____

   If you don't listen, you won't lurn.

2. Circle the correct spelling.   apear   appear

3. Correct the spelling mistake. _____

   The mucsles in my left leg really hurt.

4. Circle the correct spelling.   rhyme   ryhme

5. An antonym for **angry** is:

   ☐ funny   ☐ annoyed   ☐ pleased

6. Write the verb made when the suffix **ify** is added to:

   mummy   _____

   pure   _____

7. Write **sore** or **soar**.

   The eagle can _____ high into the sky.

8. Write an antonym for **maximum**.   m_____

9. In the dictionary, ... comes after **parallel**.

   ☐ parachute   ☐ paralysed   ☐ paradise

10. The letters in **exhibition** that give the **sh** sound are:

    ☐ it   ☐ ti   ☐ tio

11. Add an apostrophe.

    This cat homes aim is to find homes for all its cats.

12. Add an apostrophe.

    Those cats check-ups are at 10.30 am and 10.40 am.

13. Add an apostrophe.

    My cats kittens were born this morning.

14. Write **it's** or **its**.

    Before buying a pet, you should learn about _____ needs.

15. Complete the simile.

    The new pet was as mad as a _____ .

16. Write the missing word.

    A pride of _____ .

17. Circle the adverb.

    Tim's kittens cried constantly for the first few nights.

18. Circle the adverb that tells **when**.

    Tim's brother seldom plays with the kittens.

19. Circle the preposition.

    The kittens love to play in old cardboard boxes.

20. Write the conjunction. _____

    The kittens walk around Tim's legs as he prepares their food.

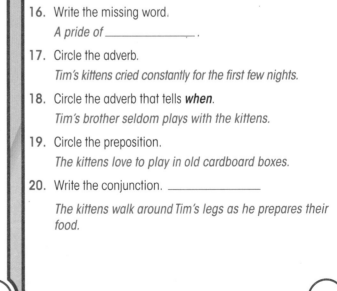

MY SCORE

MY SCORE

DAY 29

1. Correct the spelling mistake. _____

   Please turn the calender to the next month.

2. Circle the correct spelling.   inportant   important

3. Correct the spelling mistake. _____

   I never remmember to write the date on my work.

4. Circle the correct spelling.   interfere   interfear

5. A synonym for **weary** is:

   ☐ exhausted   ☐ lazy   ☐ sad

6. Write the prefix **counter** to give the opposite meaning.

   _____clockwise

7. Write as a contraction.

   were not   _____

8. Write the correct homophone. _____

   The bough/bow of the boat crashed into the bank.

9. Separate **material** into its syllables. _____

10. The plural of **fish** is _____ .

11. Add a comma to give the sentence sense.

    While the dogs were hunting the boy cleaned their kennels.

12. Add a comma.

    After cleaning the kennels he mucked out the stables.

13. Add commas to the list.

    His chores included sweeping the yard grooming the horses cleaning the stables and feeding them.

14. Write the feminine noun. _____

    In the stable, the mare nuzzled her newborn foal.

15. Circle the verbs.

    The huge bull snorted angrily as he waited and watched.

16. Circle the masculine noun.

    The mean looking black bull was ready to charge.

17. Circle the comparative adjective.

    Is bullfighting crueller than fox hunting?

18. Write the superlative adjective. _____

    'Watching the birth of the foal was the most amazing thing I've ever seen!' exclaimed Billy.

19. Another verb for **said**. _____

    You should feed it with milk,' said the vet.

20. Circle the pronoun.

    Dad winked at Billy and Lily and said the foal was theirs.

MY SCORE

DAY 30

1. Correct the spelling mistake. _____

   My cats know which cubboard their food is kept in.

2. Circle the correct spelling.   figger   figure

3. Correct the spelling mistake. _____

   When they're alone, our cats get into a lot of mischif.

4. Circle the correct spelling.   biscuit   biscit

5. An synonym for **accurate** is:

   ☐ sad   ☐ rough   ☐ precise

6. Write the noun made when the suffix **acy** is added.

   accurate   _____

   literate   _____

7. Write **quiet** and **quite** in the correct places.

   I _____ like it when the house is really

   _____ .

8. Write an antonym for **modern**.   a_____

9. In the dictionary, ... comes before **round**.

   ☐ routine   ☐ rough   ☐ route

10. In **flight**, which letters give the long **i** sound?

    ☐ i   ☐ ig   ☐ igh

11. Add an apostrophe.

    The swimmers goggles were not in his bag.

12. Add an apostrophe.

    The swimmers coach barked instructions at them.

13. Add an apostrophe.

    His swimming squads training schedule was tough.

14. Add a comma.

    To be in the squad swimmers must train every day.

15. Tick: ☐ command   ☐ question   ☐ statement

    'Shall we write our names on the squad list?'

16. Complete the simile.

    as _____ as lightning

17. Circle the adverb.

    As the alarm clock beeped, Pat groaned loudly.

18. Circle the adverb that tells **when**.

    He got up and he was soon dressed.

19. Circle the preposition.

    Training sessions are always under supervision.

20. Write the conjunction. _____

    Pat has been in the swimming squad since he joined the club.

MY SCORE

DAY 31

1. Circle the word spelt incorrectly.   vein   previde

2. Rewrite the incorrectly spelt word. _____
   charade   predater   occasion

3. Circle the correct spelling.   character   caracter

4. Rewrite the word spelt incorrectly. _____
   seize   wierd   siege

5. A synonym for **circular** is:
   ☐ argumentative ☐ round ☐ boisterous

6. The prefix **dis** (**disappear**) means:
   ☐ before ☐ against ☐ not

7. The expanded forms of **when's** are _____
   or _____ .

8. Circle the correct homophone.
   My dog always berries/buries its bone in the garden.

9. The syllables of **privilege** are _____ .

10. Write the plural of each noun.
    sky _____   day _____

11. Rewrite the phrase using an apostrophe.
    the dog of the boy
    _____

12. Circle the sentence that requires speech marks.
    I'm tired, yawned Dan.   Dan said he was tired.

13. Circle the meaning of **enhance**.
    to cut a design in glass   to increase the value

14. Circle the preposition.
    Joel delivered his party invitations after school.

15. Circle the conjunction.
    After washing his hands, Joel filled the party bags.

16. Preposition or conjunction? _____
    Food was served on the large table.

17. Circle the adjective.
    Joel invited Amy to the fantastic party.

18. Circle the adjectives.
    The happy guests said the party had been great fun.

19. Another word for **said**. _____
    Everyone said it was a great party.

20. Circle the adjectives.
    The next party will have an adventure theme.

MY SCORE

DAY 32

1. Circle the word spelt correctly.   eigthty   beauty

2. Rewrite the incorrectly spelt word. _____
   answer   tonge   yolk

3. Circle the incorrect spelling.   jeolous   jealous

4. Rewrite the incorrectly spelt word. _____
   bownce   haunted   author

5. An antonym for **humble** is: generous   conceited

6. The suffix **ish** changes the nouns to _____ .
   fiend—fiendish   fool—foolish   self—selfish

7. Write the correct word.   desert   dessert
   The camel plodded through the scorching
   _____ *sand.*

8. The word **canine** comes from
   the Latin word **canis**, meaning: ☐ cage ☐ dog

9. Alphabetically, which word follows **disturb**?
   ☐ district ☐ disqualify ☐ ditch ☐ distract

10. Circle the compound word that needs a hyphen.
    earthquake   icecream   iceberg

11. How many owners? ☐ one ☐ more than one
    the tigers' eyes

12. Circle the direct speech.
    Remember to close the gate, the zookeeper warned.

13. Complete.
    A pride of _____

14. Circle the pronoun.
    Someone left the gate to the lion enclosure open.

15. Circle the abstract noun.
    To our relief, the lions were still in there.

16. Circle the meaning of **bewilder**.
    to confuse   to live in the wild

17. Circle the correct part of the verb.
    The zookeeper was complained/complaining about visitors as he walked away.

18. Circle the correct part of the verb.
    We were keeping/kept a daily record.

19. Tick: ☐ conjunction
             ☐ preposition
    The otters were swimming in their pond.

20. Write **perform** or **performed**.
    We saw the elephants _____ *in the small arena.*

MY SCORE

1. Circle the word spelt incorrectly.   woolen   wooden
2. Rewrite the incorrectly spelt word. _____
   extreem   question   position
3. Circle the correct spelling.   excitment   excitement
4. Rewrite the word spelt incorrectly. _____
   coward   chaos   corage
5. A synonym for **conceal** is:
   ☐ hide   ☐ thicken   ☐ accept
6. The prefix **semi** (**semifinal**) means:
   ☐ half   ☐ twice   ☐ round
7. The expanded form of **I've** is _____ .
8. Circle the correct verb.
   I wandered/wondered through the park in a dream.
9. The syllables of **volcanic** are _____ .
10. Write the plural of each noun.
    pony _____   tray _____
11. Rewrite the phrase using a possessive apostrophe.
    the books of the children
    _____
12. Circle the sentence that requires speech marks.
    Eli noticed the fire.
    Look at the fire! cried Eli.
13. Circle the meaning of **intense**.
    extreme   under stress
14. Circle the verbs.
    Mum ran outside and then called the fire brigade.
15. Circle the conjunction.
    Before doing anything else, Dad made sure there was no one in the house.
16. Preposition or conjunction? _____
    The neighbours stayed well underline behind the wall for safety.
17. Circle the simile.
    The place was as hot as a furnace.
18. Circle the nouns.
    The smoke damaged the rooms inside the house.
19. Circle the adjectives.
    They were lucky to have avoided a major disaster.
20. Tick: ☐ command ☐ question ☐ statement
    Thankfully, no one was injured during the frightening event.

1. Circle the word spelt correctly.   delight   allthough
2. Rewrite the incorrectly spelt word. _____
   professional   amateur   journy
3. Circle the incorrect spelling.   disapoint   disappoint
4. Rewrite the incorrectly spelt word. _____
   niece   voyige   asteroid
5. An antonym for **reveal** is:
   ☐ arrive   ☐ hide   ☐ lose
6. The suffix **al** changes the nouns to _____ .
   fiction—fictional   magic—magical
   emotion—emotional
7. **main** or **mane**? _____
   The .... product that is exported is coffee.
8. Write an antonym for **export**.   i_____
9. Alphabetically, which word precedes **harpoon**?
   ☐ harvest ☐ harmony ☐ hassle ☐ harsh
10. Circle the compound word that needs a hyphen.
    sixteen   nineteen   thirtythree
11. How many owners?   ☐ one   ☐ more than one
    the city's traffic
12. Circle the direct speech.
    Dad groaned, I always miss the green lights!
13. Circle the adverb.
    Dad mistakenly believes that the traffic lights turn red when they see his car approaching.
14. Circle the two pronouns.
    Dad thinks traffic lights know his car; he hates them!
15. Circle the indefinite article.
    His dream is to live in a town with no traffic lights.
16. Circle the meaning of **chaos**.
    crazy panic   a country
17. Circle the correct part.
    Because Dad was/had dreaming, he missed the lights changing.
18. Circle the correct part.
    Mum was/had laughed when he told her off.
19. Tick: ☐ conjunction
          ☐ preposition
    My dad's mood changes when he gets in the car.
20. Circle the word that is not needed.
    My dad needs to relax down in the evening.

DAY 35

1. Circle the word spelt incorrectly.   hearse   nethphew

2. Rewrite the incorrectly spelt word. _____
   terific   lounge   phrase

3. Circle the correct spelling.   truthful   truethfl

4. Rewrite the word spelt incorrectly. _____
   excape   dough   heroic

5. A synonym for **shambles** is:
   ☐ disgrace   ☐ wreck   ☐ imitation

6. The prefix **inter** (**intergalactic**) means:
   ☐ across   ☐ between   ☐ above

7. The expanded form of **they're** is _____ .

8. Circle the correct homophone.
   The stationary/stationery car was hit by the branch.

9. The syllables of **identify** are _____ .

10. Write the plural of each noun.
    Friday   _____
    army   _____

11. Rewrite the phrase using an apostrophe.
    the tails of the horses
    _____

12. Circle the sentence that requires speech marks.
    Amy looked upset.   Amy wailed, I'm so upset!

13. Add commas.
    Amy needs a brush a comb a helmet and a jacket before the competition.

14. Circle the preposition.
    The brush and comb were beneath the clothes.

15. Circle the conjunction.
    She was well-rewarded for the hard work she had done.

16. Preposition or conjunction? _____
    Amy has never fallen from her horse.

17. Another word for **lovely**. _____
    The annual event was lovely.

18. Tick: ☐ command ☐ question ☐ statement
    The event was blessed with a perfect autumn day.

19. Circle the adjectives.
    People went home tired but happy after the lovely day.

20. Circle the adjectives.
    The next day, kind people helped to clear up.

DAY 36

1. Circle the word spelt correctly.   peice   brief

2. Rewrite the incorrectly spelt word. _____
   fraight   tough   quay

3. Circle the incorrect spelling.   machine   mashine

4. Rewrite the incorrectly spelt word. _____
   suspence   attack   modern

5. An antonym for **colossal** is: ☐ colourful   ☐ tiny

6. The suffix **ic** changes the nouns to _____ .
   graph—graphic   hero—heroic   ocean—oceanic

7. **sweet** or **suite**? _____
   The .... of furniture cost us a lot of money.

8. Write a synonym for **terror**.   f_____

9. Alphabetically, which word follows **sour**?
   ☐ soul   ☐ sound   ☐ soup   ☐ south

10. Circle the compound word that needs a hyphen.
    postmortem   poster   postman

11. How many owners?   ☐ one   ☐ more than one
    the women's crew

12. Circle the direct speech.
    What a great race! screamed their excited coach.

13. Add a full stop and a capital letter.
    The women's team were congratulated by the club's president for the third year in a row, they were victorious.

14. Circle the meaning of **replenish**.
    to check carefully   to fill up again

15. Another word for **said**. _____
    The women said they were exhausted.

16. Pronoun or adjective? _____
    The women had a big challenge ahead of them in the next race.

17. Circle the correct part of the verb.
    The crew was leading/led the women's division.

18. Circle the correct part of the verb.
    The coach had trained/training them very well.

19. Tick: ☐ conjunction
        ☐ preposition
    The club held a celebration beside the river.

20. Circle the mistake.
    The women's meddles lay beside the cup.

MY SCORE

MY SCORE

DAY 37

1. Circle the word spelt incorrectly.   aisle   choyce

2. Rewrite the incorrectly spelt word. _____
   early   mobile   sawce

3. Circle the correct spelling.   bravry   bravery

4. Rewrite the word spelt incorrectly. _____
   easy   weather   oshan

5. A synonym for **inquisitive** is:
   ☐ curious   ☐ disinterested   ☐ boring

6. The prefix **super** (**superpower**) means:
   ☐ under   ☐ beside   ☐ above

7. The expanded form of **shan't** is _____.

8. Circle the correct homophone.
   The company will higher/hire new workers soon.

9. The syllables of **negative** are _____.

10. Write the plural of each noun.
    monkey   _____
    fly   _____

11. Rewrite the phrase using an apostrophe.
    the roof of the house
    _____

12. Circle the sentence that requires speech marks.
    Stop thief! cried Mum.

    Mum told the thief to stop.

13. Circle the meaning of **deter.**
    to prevent   to make sure

14. Circle the verb group.
    Mum had owned that bike since she was twenty.

15. Circle the conjunction.
    Since the thief had not damaged it, Mum could still ride the bike.

16. Verb or adjective? _____
    I have been in the same cycling club as my parents since I was eight years old.

17. Circle the indefinite article.
    A man with dark hair came on our club ride today.

18. Another word for **said.** _____
    Mum said she recognised his bike.

19. Circle the definite article.
    The nervous man saw Mum looking at his fancy bike.

20. Circle the adjectives.
    The stolen bike belonged to Dad's best friend, Pete.

DAY 38

1. Circle the word spelt correctly.   speshal   queue

2. Rewrite the incorrectly spelt word. _____
   near   ocuppy   freckle

3. Circle the incorrect spelling.   prepose   propose

4. Rewrite the incorrectly spelt word. _____
   narrow   espeshly   award

5. An antonym for **insolent** is:
   ☐ soluble   ☐ polite   ☐ solvent

6. The suffix **en** changes the adjectives to _____.
   bright—brighten fresh—freshen weak—weaken

7. **steal** or **steel**? _____
   The bridge has .... and concrete parts.

8. Write an antonym for **solid**. I_____

9. Alphabetically, which word precedes **throne**?
   ☐ through   ☐ throat   ☐ throw   ☐ throttle

10. Circle the compound word that needs a hyphen.
    outline   offpeak   outrage

11. How many families?   ☐ one   ☐ more than one
    the families' joy

12. Circle the direct speech.
    The guard announced, Everyone is safe.

13. Circle the meaning of **demolish**.
    to tear down   to leave standing

14. Circle the pronoun.
    Many buildings were demolished after the earthquake as it had damaged the foundations.

15. Write **its** or **it's**.
    The city lost many of _____ old buildings on that sad day.

16. Insert **went** or **was gone**.
    Although their historic town centre _____, the spirit of the people was stronger.

17. Circle the correct part.
    The citizens had been/had discussed the loss of their old buildings for months after the event.

18. Circle the correct part.
    Builders were/had working hard to finish the job.

19. Tick: ☐ conjunction
    ☐ preposition
    The city was now better prepared for an emergency.

20. Circle the verb group.
    The disaster will be remembered for a long time.

1. Circle the word spelt incorrectly. eesily guess

2. Rewrite the incorrectly spelt word. _____
   twelfthf   weight   thorough

3. Circle the correct spelling. shouldier   shoulder

4. Rewrite the word spelt incorrectly. _____
   competition   repeat   stomick

5. A synonym for **guarded** is:
   ☐ protected ☐ imprisoned ☐ suspicious

6. The prefix **trans** (**transatlantic**) means:
   ☐ across ☐ over ☐ inside

7. The expanded form of **can't** is _____.

8. Circle the correct homophone.
   We shall cell/sell our house and move to the city.

9. The syllables of **experiment** are _____.

10. Write the plural of each noun.
    journey   _____
    ruby   _____

11. Rewrite the phrase using an apostrophe.
    the den of the lions
    _____

12. Circle the sentence that requires speech marks.
    Go away! shouted Tom.
    Tom told the dog to go away.

13. Circle the meaning of **contemplate**.
    to know the answer   to think about

14. Circle the preposition.
    Tom walked quickly through the park.

15. Circle the conjunction.
    The dog followed Tom until it saw a cat to chase.

16. Preposition or conjunction? _____
    Tom loved walking in the hills and would have carried on until midnight, if he could.

17. Circle the abstract noun.
    A stroll in the hills is Tom's greatest pleasure.

18. Insert a comma.
    On clear days Tom can see many species of birds.

19. Circle the adjectives.
    Majestic birds of prey swooped across the clear sky.

20. Circle the adjectives.
    Delicate wildflowers swayed in the gentle breeze.

1. Circle the word spelt correctly. rythm determined

2. Rewrite the incorrectly spelt word. _____
   cureiosity   caught   exercise

3. Circle the incorrect spelling. lightning lighterning

4. Rewrite the incorrectly spelt word. _____
   individual   claim   embarass

5. An antonym for **organised** is: ☐ attentive
   ☐ disorganised

6. The suffix **ary** changes the nouns to _____.
   revolution—revolutionary
   moment—momentary

7. **vain** or **vein**? _____
   The woman looking in the mirror is so ....

8. Write a synonym of **imitate**. c_____

9. Alphabetically, which word precedes **efficient**?
   ☐ effect ☐ effort ☐ effluent ☐ effigy

10. Circle the compound word that needs a hyphen.
    twentyfirst   ongoing   offspring

11. How many owners? ☐ one ☐ more than one
    the horse's hooves

12. Circle the direct speech.
    The stable boy muttered, I always get the rotten jobs.

13. Circle the meaning of **contempt**.
    to know the answer   having no respect for something

14. Circle the pronoun.
    After grooming the horses, Carl led them inside.

15. Write **they're** or **their**.
    They enjoyed the fresh hay after _____ day's work.

16. Pronoun or adjective? _____
    Carl puts the horses out in the morning to give them a free run across the field.

17. Circle the correct part of the verb.
    The horses had sleeping/slept on the clean straw.

18. Circle the correct part of the verb.
    Carl was adding/added fresh water to the trough.

19. Tick: ☐ pronoun
    ☐ preposition
    The horses scratch themselves against a post.

20. Cross out the word that does not belong.
    Carl stood against the wall and watched the horses deter.

UNIT 4

MY SCORE

MY SCORE

1. Circle the word spelt incorrectly.   busness   breathe

2. Rewrite the incorrectly spelt word. _____
   fruit   muscle   strenth

3. Circle the correct spelling.   comunity   community

4. Rewrite the word spelt incorrectly. _____
   athleat   heart   quarter

5. A synonym for **tattered** is:
   ☐ tattooed   ☐ shabby   ☐ rambling

6. In which word are the letters **en** not a prefix meaning **cause to**?
   ☐ enlarge   ☐ enforce   ☐ enough

7. The contraction in **I'd have** means _____.

8. Circle the correct homophone.
   The rabbit disappeared into the small hole/whole.

9. The syllables of **available** are _____.

10. Write the plural of each noun.
    alibi _____   taxi _____
    ski _____

11. Add the apostrophe.
    Some of my roofs tiles had been lost in the storm.

12. Circle the direct speech.
    During the storm, said Joe, we lost a few tiles from the roof.

13. Add speech marks to show the direct speech.
    Others have suffered more damage than us, murmured Joe, so we shouldn't complain.

14. Circle the two verbs.
    We went camping and we had a wonderful time.

15. Circle the conjunction.
    I like to camp in the woods, but Kai prefers the beach.

16. Circle the meaning of **provoke**.
    to anger   to challenge

17. Circle the preposition.
    Our secluded campsite among the trees was perfect.

18. Is the word **lulled** used correctly? ☐ **yes** ☐ **no**
    The sound of the crashing waves lulled us to sleep.

19. Circle the definite article.
    The forest setting was very tranquil.

20. Circle: beach   beech
    In contrast, the .... was much more vibrant.

1. Circle the word spelt incorrectly.   compleet   chaos

2. Rewrite the incorrectly spelt word. _____
   promise   strange   languige

3. Circle the incorrect spelling.   cemetry   cemetery

4. Rewrite the incorrectly spelt word. _____
   aincent   peculiar   popular

5. An antonym for **hilarious** is:
   ☐ serious   ☐ historical

6. Write the verb made when the suffix **ate** is added to the noun.
   alien   _____
   assassin   _____

7. **main** or **mane**?   _____
   The horse's .... needed to be brushed.

8. Write a synonym for **interior**.   i_____

9. Alphabetically, which word follows **feather**?
   ☐ feat   ☐ feature   ☐ fear   ☐ feast

10. Which pair of words forms a compound word?
    ☐ decimal point ☐ fire place ☐ guinea pig

11. How many owners?   ☐ one   ☐ more than one
    the children's books

12. Insert speech marks.
    I'm saving hard, said Tim, to buy a new bike.

13. Add speech marks.
    I should have enough, he continued, by the holidays.

14. Circle the preposition.
    Tim, who loved cycling, went everywhere on his bike.

15. Circle the meaning of **gesture**.
    a clown in medieval times   body movement

16. Circle the error.
    Tim, that was very competitive, really wanted to win.

17. **winning** or **won**? _____
    Tim had never .... a bike race.

18. **losing** or **lost**? _____
    After a puncture, he .... his lead and the race.

19. Circle the conjunction.
    Although he lost the race, Tim had a great day.

20. Finish the proverb.
    Every cloud has a _____ lining.

MY SCORE

MY SCORE

UNIT 5

1. Circle the word spelt incorrectly.   operation   build

2. Rewrite the incorrectly spelt word. _____
   posession   potatoes   remember

3. Circle the correct spelling.   electrical   ellectrical

4. Rewrite the word spelt incorrectly. _____
   attached   serficient   calendar

5. A synonym for **severe** is:
   ☐ many   ☐ harsh   ☐ separate

6. In which word are the letters **in** not a prefix meaning **not**?
   ☐ inadequate   ☐ ink   ☐ insane

7. The contraction in **we'd eaten** means _____ .

8. Circle the correct homophone.
   We are reading a very exciting cereal/serial in class.

9. The syllables of **probably** are _____ .

10. Write the plural of each noun.
    torch _____   bus _____
    box _____

11. Add the apostrophe.
    Time to vote now the politicians campaigns are over.

12. Circle the direct speech.
    Vote for our party, urged Dean Dare, and see the country prosper.

13. Add speech marks to show the direct speech.
    Don't be fooled, replied Clark Kane, the country deserves a better government.

14. Circle the conjunction.
    My parents went to the polls but they did not know who to vote for.

15. Circle **thinks** or **thought**.
    Dad _____ Kane was better, but Mum didn't agree.

16. Circle the meaning of **democracy**.
    elected by the people   controlled by one person

17. Another word for **said**. _____
    The politician said he would create more jobs.

18. Circle the definite article.
    The outcome of the next election will be interesting.

19. Circle the adjectives.
    Politics seems dull and boring to many people.

20. Finish the proverb.
    Better late than _____ .

MY SCORE

1. Circle the word spelt incorrectly.   weight   pysical

2. Rewrite the incorrectly spelt word. _____
   probably   experament   sacrifice

3. Circle the incorrect spelling.   modern   moddun

4. Rewrite the incorrectly spelt word. _____
   guide   explernation   sincerely

5. An antonym for **ferocious** is: ☐ gentle ☐ barren

6. The suffix **ity** changes the adjectives to _____ .
   active—activity   agile—agility   dense—density

7. **from** or **to**? _____
   Her latest novel is different .... her last three.

8. The word **dentist** comes from the Latin word
   dens meaning   ☐ thick   ☐ tooth

9. Alphabetically, _____ precedes **stile**.
   sting   stick   stitch

10. Which pair of words forms a compound word?
    ☐ sheep dip ☐ cup board ☐ prime minister

11. How many owners?   ☐ one   ☐ more than one
    the people's princess

12. Write **decided** or **argued**.
    'The health of planet Earth', _____ the scientist, 'is an insult to past and future generations.'

13. Add speech marks to show the direct speech.
    In little over 200 years, she went on, we have brought our 4-billion-year-old planet to its knees.

14. Circle the better word.   educated   explained
    People who are unaware of the environmental damage they are causing need to be ....

15. Circle the expression.
    With so much publicity, people who do not know about our choking planet must live in the clouds.

16. Circle the adverb.
    People who thoughtlessly discard plastic products should research the 'Pacific garbage patch'.

17. **solving** or **solved**? _____
    How can such a problem be .... ?

18. **forgot** or **forgotten**? _____
    Out in the ocean, the problem is easily ....

19. Circle the conjunction.
    The problem will continue until everyone takes responsibility.

20. Finish the proverb.
    Once bitten, twice _____ .

MY SCORE

UNIT 5

DAY 45

1. Circle the word spelt correctly.   revelant   forty

2. Rewrite the incorrectly spelt word. _____
   bruise   increse   definite

3. Circle the correct spelling.   brillyant   brilliant

4. Rewrite the word spelt incorrectly. _____
   natural   mention   oppertunity

5. A synonym for **courageous** is:
   ☐ strong   ☐ valiant   ☐ messenger

6. In which word are the letters **fore** not a prefix meaning **before**?
   ☐ forecast   ☐ foreground   ☐ forest

7. The contraction in **what'd happen** means _____ .

8. Circle the correct homophone.
   I pored/poured milk on my muesli.

9. The syllables of **dictionary** are _____ .

10. Write the plural of each noun.
    studio _____   radio _____
    patio _____

11. Add the apostrophe.
    The writers books were displayed beside their photos.

12. Circle the direct speech.
    Writing a book, began Sophie, can be challenging.

13. Add speech marks to show the direct speech.
    My first book, Sophie added, took the longest to write.

14. Circle the conjunction.
    Many people believe they could write a successful novel yet few have achieved it.

15. Circle the word that is not needed.
    Sophie finished her first novel when she was 18 yet it was five years before since it was published.

16. Circle the meaning of the word **dictator**.
    person who governs by his/her own rules
    person who writes down what you said

17. Circle the adverb.
    Ideas for stories may come to me quite unexpectedly.

18. Circle the indefinite article.
    Many successful authors write to a formula.

19. Circle the adjectives.
    Writing sounds like an exciting if insecure career.

20. Finish the proverb.
    Out of sight, out of _____ .

DAY 46

1. Circle the word spelt incorrectly.   sinserely   heard

2. Rewrite the incorrectly spelt word. _____
   resteront   suggest   desperate

3. Circle the incorrect spelling.   knowlidge   knowledge

4. Rewrite the incorrectly spelt word. _____
   caught   naughty   preistoric

5. An antonym for **friendly** is: ☐ hostile ☐ indifferent

6. Add the suffix **ive** to these verbs.
   attract _____   select _____

7. **bad** or **badly**? _____
   I felt I had done .... in my test but I scored 100%!

8. The word **primary** comes from the Latin word **prima** meaning   ☐ first   ☐ tooth

9. Alphabetically, _____ follows **various**.
   variety   varnish   variable

10. Which pair of words forms a compound word?
    ☐ bush band   ☐ air force   ☐ care taker

11. How many owners?   ☐ one   ☐ more than one
    the geese's shelter

12. Add speech marks.
    When I'm older, stated Chloe, I will be an acrobat.

13. Add speech marks to show the direct speech.
    Acrobatics, she continued, is in my blood.

14. Write **that** or **who**.
    Chloe, _____ has been interested in acrobatics since she was very young, has two brothers.

15. Circle the proper adjective.
    Chloe, who has a Swiss coach, is 10 years old.

16. Circle the correct meaning of **technique**.
    a way of doing something   a strange event

17. **fell** or **fallen**? _____
    In one routine, Chloe had .... and hurt herself.

18. **broke** or **broken**? _____
    She was thankful not to have .... any bones.

19. Circle the conjunction.
    Whenever Chloe falls, her mum closes her eyes.

20. Finish the proverb.
    Birds of a feather _____ .

MY SCORE

MY SCORE

1. Circle the word spelt incorrectly.   group   inough

2. Rewrite the incorrectly spelt word. _____
   matterial   awkward   neighbour

3. Circle the correct spelling.   signiture   signature

4. Rewrite the word spelt incorrectly. _____
   dictionary   dissapear   sacrifice

5. A synonym for **dangerous** is:
   ⬭ hazardous   ⬭ difficult   ⬭ boring

6. In which word are the letters **de** not a prefix meaning **the opposite**?
   ⬭ delicate   ⬭ deflate   ⬭ decrease

7. The contraction in **who'd seen** means _____ .

8. Circle the correct homophone.
   The sight/site for the new house is perfect.

9. The syllables of **opportunity** are _____ .

10. Write the plural of each noun.
    buffalo _____   echo _____
    torpedo _____

11. Add the apostrophe.
    South Americas history is steeped in ancient traditions and colonial violence.

12. Circle the direct speech.
    Machu Picchu, droned the guide, is 600 years old.

13. Add speech marks to show the direct speech.
    The Spanish invaders, he added, were unaware of its existence.

14. Circle the proper adjective.
    The Spanish invaders didn't discover Machu Picchu so it was not plundered like other sacred sites.

15. Circle the conjunction.
    Machu Picchu is a popular tourist destination so now it faces a different kind of danger.

16. Circle the meaning of the word **plunder**.
    to cause great damage   a tool that a plumber uses

17. Circle the verb.
    The discovery of ancient sites is always exciting.

18. Circle the definite article.
    The history of ancient empires is important to us.

19. Circle the adjectives.
    The Incas had an educated, well-governed society.

20. Finish the proverb.
    A bird in the hand is worth _____ .

1. Circle the word spelt incorrectly.   vacinate   occasion

2. Rewrite the incorrectly spelt word. _____
   amateur   alpherbet   particular

3. Circle the incorrect spelling.   energy   enegy

4. Rewrite the incorrectly spelt word. _____
   pehraps   important   experiment

5. An antonym for **flexible** is: ⬭ difficult   ⬭ rigid

6. Add the suffix **ly** to make adverbs.
   happy _____   angry _____

7. **lay** or **lie**? _____
   I need to .... down and rest for a while.

8. Write a synonym for **exterior**.   o_____

9. Alphabetically, _____ precedes **beard**.
   beast   beauty   beacon

10. Which pair of words forms a compound word?
    ⬭ leg room   ⬭ note book   ⬭ food chain

11. How many owners?   ⬭ one   ⬭ more than one
    the nation's buried mummies

12. Add speech marks.
    A peat bog, began Mr Hill, is an oxygen-free wetland.

13. Add speech marks to show the direct speech.
    Such a place, he continued, is perfect for mummification.

14. Write **interesting** or **interested**.
    Scientists are _____ in people who have been discovered in peat bogs.

15. Circle the word that is not needed.
    Scientists who will have examined the mummies say most had suffered violent deaths.

16. Circle the prepositions.
    We learn about prehistory from scientists.

17. **broke** or **broken**? _____
    After his death, Lindow Man's neck was ....

18. **took** or **taken**? _____
    The mummies have been .... from the bogs.

19. Circle the conjunction.
    The full truth is unknown because there is no written evidence.

20. Finish the proverb.
    All's well that _____ .

UNIT 5

MY SCORE

MY SCORE

DAY 49

1. Circle the word spelt incorrectly.   perpose   occupy

2. Rewrite the incorrectly spelt word. _____
   century   temperture   disastrous

3. Circle the correct spelling.   disability   disabilerty

4. Rewrite the word spelt incorrectly. _____
   exercise   natural   sootcase

5. A synonym for **abundant** is:
   ☐ ample   ☐ abandon   ☐ abound

6. In which word are the letters **mid** not a prefix meaning **the middle**?
   ☐ midweek   ☐ midwinter   ☐ midge

7. The contraction in **how'd you feel** means _____ .

8. Circle the correct homophone.
   The ship docked at the key/quay an hour late.

9. The syllables of **disastrous** are _____ .

10. Write the plural of each noun.
    solo _____   zero _____
    avocado _____

11. Add the apostrophe.
    Marcel Marceau was one of Frances great heroes.

12. Circle the direct speech.
    At the age of 84, said the newsreader, the mime artist and war hero, Marcel Marceau, has died.

13. Add speech marks to show the direct speech.
    Marcel Marceau, he continued, will always be remembered for his character, 'Bip' the clown.

14. Write **during or since.**
    Marcel joined the French Resistance _____ the war and helped many Jews escape from the Germans.

15. Circle the conjunction.
    Marcel was a great comedian and he studied acting after the war.

16. Circle the meaning of the word **renowned**.
    celebrated or famous
    something that happens in the present

17. Circle the proper adjective.
    This famous French mime artist died in 2007.

18. Circle the definite article.
    The French Resistance movement worked undercover.

19. Insert a suitable adjective.
    The face of 'Bip' the clown was ghostly _____ .

20. Finish the proverb.
    When the cat's away _____ .

DAY 50

1. Circle the word spelt correctly.   riegn   appear

2. Rewrite the incorrectly spelt word. _____
   actually   although   veggterble

3. Circle the incorrect spelling.   coastul   coastal

4. Rewrite the incorrectly spelt word. _____
   regular   assemberly   describe

5. An antonym for **artificial** is:
   ☐ authentic   ☐ synthetic

6. The suffix **ly** changes the adjectives to _____ .
   spiteful—spitefully   normal—normally

7. **vain** or **vein**? _____
   Your .... carries blood.

8. Write an antonym for **captivity**.   f_____

9. Alphabetically, _____ precedes **journey**.
   jovial   joust   jostle

10. Which pair of words forms a compound word?
    ☐ rain forest   ☐ gas fire   ☐ riding boots

11. How many owners?   ☐ one   ☐ more than one
    sharks' distress

12. Add speech marks.
    Shark finning, Ali began, should be banned.

13. Add speech marks to show the direct speech.
    When sharks are caught, she said, their fins are cut off and the sharks are thrown back in the water.

14. The underlined word is a: ☐ noun   ☐ verb
    I think people who eat shark soup are selfish.

15. Write **is** or **are**.
    People who buy shark fins _____ greedy.

16. Circle the word that is not needed.
    I think people who catch really protected sharks are criminals.

17. **threw** or **thrown**? _____
    The sharks are .... back overboard to die.

18. **spending** or **spent**? _____
    Last month, restaurants .... a lot of money on shark fins.

19. Circle the conjunction.
    Unless laws are enforced, protected species will become extinct.

20. Finish the proverb.
    Every cloud _____ .

1. Correct the spelling.   binocculers   _____

2. Correct the spelling.   sissers   _____

3. Correct the spelling.   cellarbrate   _____

4. Correct the spelling.   dinersaur   _____

5. A synonym for **ambitious** is:
   ☐ driving   ☐ driven   ☐ ambidextrous

6. In which word are the letters **pre** a prefix meaning **before**?
   ☐ precise   ☐ precaution   ☐ precious

7. The contraction in **Tom's going** means _____ .

8. Circle the correct homophone.
   The <u>air/heir</u> to the throne was just a child.

9. Circle the word with more syllables.   delicious   famous

10. Add **ed** to give the past participle of each verb.
    carry _____   copy _____
    bury _____

11. There: ☐ are two sentences.
    ☐ is one sentence.
    'We had already searched for five years', said Carter. 'We decided to try for just one more year.'

12. The underlined is followed by a:
    ☐ comma ☐ full stop
    'It is quite amazing', <u>he laughed</u> 'We could have given up and the tomb may never have been found!'

13. Add a **full stop** or **comma**.
    'The tomb lay undisturbed for 3000 years', Carter marvelled☐ 'Many others have been plundered.'

14. Circle the proper nouns.
    Before he located the tomb of Tutankhamen, Howard Carter had found the tomb of Queen Hatshepsut.

15. Insert the correct form of **thief**.
    Even though they had been sealed, many royal tombs had been raided by _____ .

16. Circle a phrase that means **renowned**.
    Howard Carter became world famous once he had discovered the young king's tomb.

17. Circle the word that means **written onto**.
    A warning to thieves was engraved on the tomb.

18. Circle the verb group.
    Later, Carter's pet was eaten by a cobra.

19. Circle the preposition.
    Lord Carnarvon had a mosquito bite on his cheek.

20. Circle the abstract noun.
    Carnarvon's dog died in great distress.

1. Correct the spelling.   tramperline   _____

2. Correct the spelling.   mosskeyto   _____

3. Correct the spelling.   allmost   _____

4. Correct the spelling.   cumfertable   _____

5. An antonym for **risky** is: ☐ dangerous ☐ safe

6. Circle the example in which the suffix **en** does not change a noun to an adjective.
   eat—eaten   gold—golden   wood—wooden

7. **currant** or **current**? _____
   The sea had a strong and dangerous ....

8. The word **population** comes from the Latin word **populus** meaning   ☐ many   ☐ people

9. Listed alphabetically, the first word is _____ .
   learn   leave   league   lease

10. Which word does not belong in the group?
    lion   panther   tiger   zebra

11. There: ☐ are two sentences.
    ☐ is one sentence.
    'A pilgrimage is a journey to a special place', said the teacher. 'This tradition is thousands of years old.'

12. The underlined is followed by a: ☐ capital letter.
    ☐ lower-case letter.
    'The oldest known pilgrimage site is in Tibet', <u>she said</u>. 'Many Buddhists make this journey.'

13. Add a **capital S** or a **small s**.
    'The first Christian pilgrim was Helena', the teacher continued. '___he was Emperor Constantine's mother.'

14. The underlined word tells you:
    ☐ which one   ☐ which ones
    <u>This</u> hotel is for pilgrims on the 'Way of St James'.

15. Add.   This   These
    _____ pilgrimage has many starting points.

16. Add.   this   these
    Most of _____ starting points are in France.

17. Add.   less   several
    People make pilgrimages for _____ reasons.

18. Insert a suitable adjective.
    Lots of travellers find the journey very _____ .

19. Add.   many   some
    The pilgrimage can bring _____ hardship to weary travellers.

20. Select the correct word.
    Towns along the way have lots of places for <u>this/these</u> pilgrims to stay.

MY SCORE

MY SCORE

UNIT 6

DAY 53

1. Correct the spelling.   indercate   _____
2. Correct the spelling.   calculater   _____
3. Correct the spelling.   autermatic   _____
4. Correct the spelling.   recogniseable   _____
5. A synonym for **approve** is:
   ☐ accept   ☐ reject   ☐ appoint
6. In which word are the letters **un** a prefix meaning **not**?
   ☐ uncle   ☐ uniform   ☐ unnatural
7. The contraction in **Dad's gone too** means _____ .
8. Circle the correct homophone.
   The cent/scent from the flowers is beautiful.
9. Circle the word with more syllables. nervous   serious
10. Add **er** to give the comparative form of each adjective.
    weary _____   easy _____
11. There: ☐ are two sentences.
             ☐ is one sentence.
    'Before television', said the presenter, 'people knew very little about the wildlife of distant countries'.
12. The underlined is followed by a:
    ☐ comma. ☐ full stop.
    'Can you imagine', he asked 'not knowing about penguins, polar bears, crocodiles and orangutans?'
13. Add a **full stop** or **comma**.
    'For over 60 years', he said ☐ 'we have learnt about Earth's natural history from Sir David Attenborough'.
14. Circle the indefinite article.
    Because of people like Jacques Cousteau, we have learnt a lot about life in the oceans.
15. Circle the word which means **sea**.
    Before everyone had televisions, few people knew what many marine creatures looked like.
16. Circle the conjunction.
    Jacques Cousteau changed this when he began filming marine life for television documentaries.
17. The underlined word is a _____ .
    Jacques Cousteau came from south-west France.
18. Circle the abstract noun.
    He worked with great passion to protect ocean life.
19. The expression **put one's foot in it** means:
    ☐ to step into something disgusting.
    ☐ to cause embarrassment by saying the wrong thing.
20. Another verb for **said**. _____
    The historian said that Jacques Cousteau died in 1997.

MY SCORE

DAY 54

1. Correct the spelling.   conternant   _____
2. Correct the spelling.   longditude   _____
3. Correct the spelling.   exageration   _____
4. Correct the spelling.   moltiply   _____
5. An antonym for **quit** is: ☐ leave   ☐ continue
6. Circle the two words which can take the suffix **ful**.
   attract   fear   wonder
7. **its** or **it's**?
   The cow is swishing _____ tail.
8. The word **feminine** comes from the Latin word **femina** meaning: ☐ free   ☐ woman
9. Listed alphabetically, the final word is _____ .
   dollar   doctor   dolphin   document
10. Which word does not belong in the group?
    ☐ fish   ☐ frog   ☐ newt   ☐ toad
11. There: ☐ are two sentences.
             ☐ is one sentence.
    'Before deciding to have a pet', said the vet, 'it is important to know what your responsibilities will be'.
12. The underlined is followed by a: ☐ capital letter.
                                     ☐ lower-case letter.
    'When you make the decision to have a pet', she added, 'you commit to taking proper care of it'.
13. Add a **capital L** or a **lower-case l**.
    'So many people', she sighed, '☐ose interest in their pet quickly and do not look after it'.
14. The underlined word tells you:
    ☐ which one.   ☐ which ones.
    That cat prowls the neighbourhood at night.
15. Add.   that   those
    I think it prefers _____ garden to any other.
16. Add.   that   those
    My cats have always preferred _____ biscuits.
17. Circle the adverb.
    At night, you can often hear some cats fighting.
18. Add.   Much   More
    _____ people are keeping their cats in at night.
19. Add.   any   enough
    Should _____ cats be prowling the streets at night?
20. The expression **throw in the towel** means:
    ☐ to give up.   ☐ to do the laundry in a hurry.

MY SCORE

DAY 55

1. Correct the spelling. flexable _____

2. Correct the spelling. horrable _____

3. Correct the spelling. visable _____

4. Correct the spelling. sensable _____

5. A synonym for **bashful** is:
   ☐ timely   ☐ angry   ☐ timid

6. In which word are the letters **sub** not a prefix meaning **under**?
   ☐ submerge   ☐ subway   ☐ subtle

7. The contraction in **where'll you go** means
   _____.

8. Circle the correct homophone.
   Sandpaper is a coarse/course material.

9. Circle the word
   with more syllables.   ambitious   conscious

10. Add **est** to give the superlative form of each adjective.
    chewy _____   cheeky _____

11. There: ☐ are two sentences.
           ☐ is one sentence.
    'Plants and animals have natural defences', said Mr Jones. 'They help to protect them from predators.'

12. The underlined is followed by a: ☐ comma. ☐ full stop.
    'Some plants are poisonous if eaten', he said 'Others can give you a nasty sting if touched.'

13. Add a **full stop** or **comma**.
    'Never eat apple seeds', continued Mr Jones ☐ 'They contain poison which will make you sick.'

14. Circle the word meaning **poison**.
    Although venom is used in nature to harm, it can be used as medicine to help.

15. Circle the word that is not needed.
    People can die after they have been bitten or stung by a non venomous creature.

16. Circle the conjunction.
    Learning first aid is a good idea so that you would know what to do in an emergency.

17. The underlined word is a _____.
    Venom was used as a medicine in the ancient world.

18. Circle the abstract noun.
    The jellyfish in his wetsuit caused pain for Zane.

19. Circle the pronoun.
    He tore off the suit and cried in agony.

20. The expression **hit the nail on the head** means:
    ☐ to be completely correct.
    ☐ to hammer a nail into the wood in one go.

DAY 56

1. Correct the spelling. forwerd _____

2. Correct the spelling. widesbread _____

3. Correct the spelling. heartayche _____

4. Correct the spelling. floorbored _____

5. An antonym for **proud** is: ☐ ashamed ☐ prickly

6. Circle the word which can take the suffix **ment**.
   enjoy   happy   reflect

7. **passed** or **past**? _____
   Turn right after you have .... the library.

8. The word **liberty** comes from the Latin word **libera** meaning ☐ free   ☐ library

9. Listed alphabetically, the last word is _____.
   servant   serious   serpent   series

10. Which word does not belong in the group?
    ☐ dolphin ☐ seal ☐ shark ☐ whale

11. There: ☐ are two sentences.
           ☐ is one sentence.
    'A healthy lifestyle requires two things', said the instructor. 'Exercise daily and eat a balanced diet.'

12. The underlined is followed by a: ☐ capital letter.
                                      ☐ lower-case letter.
    'Exercise does not have to mean playing sport', she said. 'It includes gardening or housework.'

13. Add a **capital Y** or a **lower-case y**.
    'Most of your food should be nutritious', she continued. '☐ou can still enjoy the occasional treat!'

14. The underlined word tells you: ☐ how much.
                                     ☐ how many.
    I drink more water in summer than in winter.

15. Circle.   less   little
    Mum drinks .... coffee now than she used to.

16. Circle.   any   plenty of
    Grandad gets .... rest during the day.

17. The underlined word tells you:
    ☐ which one.   ☐ which ones.
    These water bottles belong to me.

18. Circle.   this   these
    Mum has changed to .... flavour of herbal tea.

19. Circle.   This   These
    .... armchairs by the fire are Grandad's favourites.

20. The expression **in the same boat** means:
    ☐ in the same situation.   ☐ in big trouble.

MY SCORE

MY SCORE

1. Correct the spelling.   deliteful   _____
2. Correct the spelling.   imagernation   _____
3. Correct the spelling.   wellcome   _____
4. Correct the spelling.   untill   _____
5. A synonym for *cease* is: ☐ more ☐ less ☐ stop
6. *air* or *heir*? _____

   The mountain .... was cold and dry.
7. The contraction in *what'd happened* means _____ .
8. Circle the correct homophone.

   *The truck towed away **hour/our** car after the crash.*
9. Circle the word with more syllables.

   anxious   suspicious
10. Add *ed* to give the past participle of each verb.

    cry _____   try _____

    fry _____
11. There: ☐ are two sentences.
    ☐ is one sentence.

    'The human body', said the doctor, 'is an amazing, intelligent machine'.
12. The underlined is followed by a:
    ☐ comma.   ☐ full stop.

    'As well as working efficiently', <u>he added</u> 'it knows how to fix itself when something does go wrong'.
13. Add a *full stop* or *comma*.

    'Blood is the body's transport system', he said ☐ *'delivering nutrients and collecting waste'.*
14. Is the underlined word a pronoun? ☐ yes ☐ no

    When you fall off your bike, you may bruise <u>yourself</u>.
15. Circle the word that is not needed.

    A bruise can forms when the blood vessels under the skin are damaged.
16. Circle the conjunction.

    A bruise can change from red to purple to yellow until the skin returns to its normal colour.
17. The underlined word is a _____ .

    A scab <u>forms</u> on cut skin to protect the wound while new skin forms.
18. Circle the preposition.

    Platelets in the blood make it sticky so a scab forms.
19. The expression *sit on the fence* means:

    ☐ to actually sit on a fence.

    ☐ to avoid taking sides in an argument.
20. The word *dwindle* means:

    ☐ to shrink gradually.

    ☐ to be powerful and energetic.

1. Correct the spelling.   spagetti   _____
2. Correct the spelling.   paragrarph   _____
3. Correct the spelling.   apoinnt   _____
4. Correct the spelling.   dervide   _____
5. An antonym for *prevent* is: ☐ allow ☐ definite
6. Circle the two words which can take the suffix *ness*.

   bitter   attract   happy
7. *steal* or *steel*? _____

   The thief tried to .... the diamond necklace.
8. The word *location* comes from the Latin word *locus*
   meaning   ☐ locust   ☐ place
9. Listed alphabetically, the third word is _____ .

   profit   prohibit   progress   project
10. Which word does not belong in the group?
    ☐ calf ☐ bear ☐ cub ☐ foal
11. There: ☐ are two sentences.
    ☐ is one sentence.

    'Landscape gardening', agreed Dad, 'would be a great career to get into'.
12. The underlined is followed by a: ☐ capital letter.
    ☐ lower-case letter.

    'You'd have to learn all about plants', <u>he added</u>, 'and the different types of soils'.
13. Add a *capital D* or a *lower-case d*.

    'If I could change my career', he sighed, ' ☐ *esigning and building gardens would be what I'd choose'.*
14. Complete the sentence using a simile.

    That lawnmower is as _____ as a razor.
15. Add.   That   Those

    _____ *plants by the tree will be better than these.*
16. Circle the preposition.

    This plant will look good between those bushes.
17. The word *scant* means:

    a small amount   to look quickly
18. Add.   Both   Every

    _____ *plant will be used in the rockery.*
19. Circle the correct word.   few   some

    Plants will trail over .... rocks like a waterfall.
20. The expression *mind your p's and q's* means:

    ☐ be careful about your handwriting and spelling.

    ☐ be careful about your actions and behaviour.

MY SCORE

MY SCORE

UNIT 6

1. Correct the spelling.   intervyoo   _____
2. Correct the spelling.   submerine   _____
3. Correct the spelling.   astaroid   _____
4. Correct the spelling.   frekkle   _____
5. A synonym for **dormant** is:
   ☐ sleeping   ☐ winter   ☐ tired
6. In which word are the letters **mis** a prefix meaning **wrongly**?
   ☐ miserable   ☐ mischief   ☐ mislead
7. The contraction **could've** means _____ .
8. Circle the correct homophone.
   The wound will heal/heel but it may leave a scar.
9. Circle the word with more syllables.   curious   precious
10. Add **es** to give the simple present tense for **he**, **she**, **it**.
    bully _____   hurry _____
    spy _____
11. There: ☐ are two sentences.
            ☐ is one sentence.
    'Summer camp this year will be in a forest', said Mr Betts. 'Water sports will be included on a lake.'
12. The underlined is followed by a:
    ☐ comma.   ☐ full stop.
    'Activities will include canoeing', he said 'You will need to master the Eskimo roll.'
13. Add a **full stop** or **comma**.
    'Everyone will wear a life jacket', continued Mr Betts ☐ 'There will be no exceptions to this rule.'
14. Circle the pronoun.
    You will not take part in the canoeing activity unless you are wearing a life jacket.
15. This sentence is in the _____ tense.
    Our group will canoe while yours will orienteer.
16. Circle the conjunction.
    Before we have breakfast each day, we will all take a walk around the lake.
17. The underlined word is an _____ .
    We will be away for four days and three nights.
18. Circle the preposition.
    The camp huts are beside the lake.
19. The expression **let the cat out of the bag** means:
    ☐ tell something which should be a secret.
    ☐ disappoint your family by your actions.
20. The word **herbivore** means:
    ☐ an animal that eats meat.
    ☐ an animal that eats plants.

1. Correct the spelling.   eightth   _____
2. Correct the spelling.   festerval   _____
3. Correct the spelling.   photergraph   _____
4. Correct the spelling.   straigt   _____
5. An antonym for **optional** is: ☐ maybe ☐ compulsory
6. Circle the two words that can take the suffix **ous**.
   danger   misery   fame
7. **They're**, **Their** or **There**? _____
   .... *are no strawberries left for me!*
8. Write a synonym for **odour**.   s_____
9. Listed alphabetically, the second word is _____ .
   frieze   friend   friction   fright
10. Which word does not belong in the group?
    ☐ milk   ☐ juice   ☐ cheese   ☐ water
11. There: ☐ are two sentences.
            ☐ is one sentence.
    'Eating out is a great treat', said Mum. 'People cook for you and then clear up afterwards!'
12. The underlined is followed by a: ☐ capital letter.
                                     ☐ lower-case letter.
    'It's not just the food and service I notice', Mum went on. 'The surroundings are important too.'
13. Add a **capital** or a **lower-case i**.
    'Hygiene is the most important thing for me', she continued. '☐f a place looks dirty, I won't eat there.'
14. Add.   this   that
    This cafe looks better than _____ one over there.
15. Add **these** and **those**.
    _____ chairs by the window look hard but
    _____ here look more comfortable.
16. Add.   this   these
    This bread is soft but _____ chips aren't.
17. Add.   That   Those
    _____ curtains are too short for that window.
18. Add.   several   a few
    I have eaten at _____ restaurants
    but only _____ have been excellent.
19. Write the better word.   some   enough
    There is _____ money left for dessert but not enough for a tip.
20. Add.   a little   plenty of
    There is only _____ cake left but _____ ice-cream.

MY SCORE

MY SCORE

DAY 61

1. Circle the correct spelling. vicious vitious

2. Circle the correct spelling. protien protein

3. Add the silent letter. dou___t

4. Circle the correct spelling. adoreable adorable

5. A synonym for **achieve** is:
   ☐ sneeze ☐ gain ☐ ache

6. In which word do the letters **com** mean **together**?
   ☐ combine ☐ comment ☐ comma

7. The contraction of **might not** is _____ .

8. Circle the correct homophone.
   The film starts at half-<u>past/passed</u> five.

9. Circle the word with fewer syllables. celestial martial

10. Rewrite each word with **ing** added.
    carry _____ die _____
    ride _____

11. Add one comma to this sentence.
    At the side of the road the child sat crying.

12. Enclose the additional information in commas.
    Julie a champion skater is my sister's friend.

13. Add commas to the sentence.
    The children's menu gave a choice: chicken nuggets pizza and fish all served with french fries mash or salad.

14. Circle the missing pronoun. I you he she it
    When Mum cooks dinner, ... asks me to help.

15. Circle the missing pronoun. we you they
    When my parents have finished dinner, ... go for a walk.

16. Circle the noun the pronoun refers to.
    I stay with my sister and <u>she</u> helps me clean the kitchen.

17. Write the missing pronoun.
    When _____ come home, my parents play cards with us.

18. Add the present tense of the verb **to play**.
    Dad is very competitive and he always _____ to win.

19. Add the past tense of the verb **to teach**.
    Dad's father _____ him lots of different card games.

20. Add the correct part of the verb **to play**.
    _____ cards is a great way to have fun with the family.

DAY 62

1. Circle the correct spelling. ambicious ambitious

2. Circle the correct spelling. seige siege

3. Add the silent letter. i___land

4. Circle the correct spelling. possibley possibly

5. An antonym for **arrive** is: ☐ stay ☐ leave

6. Add the suffix **ial** to **industry**. _____

7. **currant** or **current**? _____
   The electrical .... is very dangerous.

8. Write an antonym for **fresh**. s_____

9. Listed alphabetically, the last word is _____ .
   circle cinder circus cinema

10. Which word does not belong in the group?
    ☐ London ☐ Texas ☐ Dublin ☐ Rome

11. Circle the speaker and the words spoken.
    Sophie cried angrily, 'I want to stay up late!'

12. Add punctuation.
    She spoke defiantly to her parents I will not go to bed

13. Add punctuation.
    Sophie tried the soft approach and said Please may I stay up a little later

14. Write the adverb telling how often. _____
    On school days, Tony always gets out of bed reluctantly.

15. Circle the adverb.
    At a snail's pace, he staggers clumsily to the bathroom.

16. **Yours** is referring to _____ .
    That toothbrush is mine, Tony. Yours is in your wash bag.

17. Circle the adjectives.
    Tony might be older, but I am taller.

18. Circle and write the compound noun. _____
    Tony walks to school as he usually misses the school bus.

19. Circle the proper noun.
    My dear brother Tony is very popular among the teachers.

20. Circle the pronouns.
    He helps the younger children at lunch time and the teachers appreciate it.

UNIT 7

MY SCORE

MY SCORE

1. Circle the correct spelling. precious   pretious
2. Circle the correct spelling. sieze   seize
3. Add the silent letter. lam___
4. Circle the correct spelling. changeable   changable
5. A synonym for **blend** is:
   ⬜ disappear   ⬜ bless   ⬜ mix
6. In which word do the letters **pro** mean a prefix joined to another word?
   ⬜ propose   ⬜ pronoun   ⬜ project
7. The contraction of **would not** is _____ .
8. Circle the correct homophone.
   Dad guessed/guest the surprise for his birthday.
9. Circle the word with fewer syllables.
   essential   special
10. Rewrite each word with **ing** added.
    hit _____   tie _____
11. Add one comma.
    Before the clock struck midnight the princess disappeared.
12. Enclose the additional information in commas.
    Arthur rode his bike a Peugeot 531 to school each day.
13. Add commas to the sentence.
    The sports available were: swimming tennis or badminton netball or basketball and cricket or baseball.
14. Circle the missing pronoun. I you he she it
    When Uncle Max sees his friends, ... tells them jokes.
15. Circle the missing pronoun. we   you   they
    When .... visit him, my sister and I laugh at his jokes.
16. Circle the noun the pronoun refers to.
    My cousin Sam is like his Dad as he also tells jokes.
17. Write the missing pronoun.
    Uncle Max and Sam are funny and _____ make us laugh.
18. Add the present tense of the verb **to visit**.
    My sister and I _____ Uncle Max and Sam on Fridays.
19. Add the past tense of the verb **to go**.
    Last Friday, we _____ to a leisure park.
20. Add the correct part of the verb **to swim**.
    I had never _____ in an outdoor pool.

1. Circle the correct spelling. caucious   cautious
2. Circle the correct spelling. chief   cheif
3. Add the silent letter. solem___
4. Circle the correct spelling. horribley   horribly
5. An antonym for **believe** is ⬜ trust ⬜ doubt
6. Add the suffix **ant** to **serve**. _____
7. **currants** or **currents**? _____
   The cake is full of .... and raisins.
8. Write a synonym for **feeble**. w_____
9. Listed alphabetically, the first word is _____ .
   deputy   desert   depend   descent
10. Which word does not belong in the group?
    ⬜ Thames ⬜ Mississippi ⬜ Nile ⬜ Pacific
11. Circle the speaker and the words spoken.
    The voice came as a whisper, 'What are you doing in my house?'
12. Add punctuation.
    Greta stuttered a reply I thought it was derelict Please forgive me.
13. Add punctuation.
    The hoarse voice answered I will but only because I am your great-great-grandmother.
14. Circle and write the adverb.
    _____
    The kittens played joyfully in the boxes.
15. Circle and write the adverb that tells when.
    _____
    They won't be so happy tomorrow, after their trip to the vet.
16. Write **their, there** or **they're**.
    The kitten in that box over _____ has caught several mice.
17. Circle the verb group.
    This kitten here has been stuck on the roof a few times.
18. Circle and write the masculine noun. _____
    Late at night, the tomcat starts to hiss and scratch the tree.
19. Circle the collective noun.
    The kittens were frightened by a flock of birds on the lawn.
20. Circle the conjunction.
    The kittens are quite naughty but they are very cute.

UNIT 7

MY SCORE

MY SCORE

1. Circle the correct spelling.   delicious   delitious
2. Circle the correct spelling.   caffeine   kaffiene
3. Add the silent letter.   lis___en
4. Circle the correct spelling.   noticeable   noticable
5. A synonym for **certain** is:
   ☐ definite   ☐ maybe   ☐ possible
6. In which word are the letters **en** not a prefix meaning **put into**?
   ☐ entangle   ☐ energy   ☐ endanger
7. The contraction of **shall not** is _____ .
8. Circle the correct homophone.
   Have you heard/herd the news about the Olympics?
9. Circle the word with fewer syllables.   initial   social
10. Rewrite each word with **ing** added.
    stop _____   lie _____
11. Add one comma.
    With a sinking feeling in his heart the player left the pitch.
12. Enclose the additional information in commas.
    The team we were playing Star Lakers forfeited the match.
13. Add commas to the sentence.
    The choices for the party included bowling watersports laser games and disco with food as an optional extra.
14. Circle the missing pronoun.   I   you   he   she   it
    Please come and see me as soon as .... get here.
15. Circle the missing pronoun.   we   you   they
    If I don't answer the door, ... will find me in the garden.
16. Circle the nouns the pronoun refers to.
    I hope Tim and Joe come too as they are very strong.
17. Write the missing pronoun.
    Dad will be pleased as _____ needs all the help we can give.
18. Add the present tense of the verb **to be**.
    Dad _____ so happy that you _____ here to help him.
19. Add the past tense of the verb **to build**.
    Last time he _____ something, it was a disaster.
20. Add the correct part of the verb **to follow**.
    _____ instructions is not his strong point!

1. Circle the correct spelling.   infeccious   infectious
2. Circle the correct spelling.   theif   thief
3. Add the silent letter.   ___night
4. Circle the correct spelling.   terribley   terribly
5. An antonym for **confess** is   ☐ deny   ☐ admit
6. Add the suffix **ial** to **testimony**. _____
7. **devise** or **device**? _____
   The bomb was a small .... concealed in a parcel.
8. Write an antonym for **public**.   p_____
9. Listed alphabetically, the second word is _____ .
   emperor   embalm   embers   emerge
10. Which word does not belong in the group?
    ☐ Amazon   ☐ Gobi   ☐ Sahara   ☐ Kalahari
11. Circle the speaker and the words spoken.
    The General spoke excitedly to his troops, 'Just one more push, boys, and we'll be through enemy lines!'
12. Add punctuation.
    A young corporal spoke up bravely Do you think I'll live to see my newborn son sir
13. Add punctuation.
    The General replied This will be your last time facing the enemy
14. Circle and write the adverb. _____
    It is always windy when I ride my bike along the coast.
15. Circle the pronoun.
    I cycle for half an hour then turn around and cycle home.
16. Circle the error.
    I enjoy cycling because it's good exercise for me?
17. Circle the verbs.
    I stop at the top of every hill and have a rest.
18. How many nouns? ☐
    I take two bottles of water and a snack on each ride.
19. How many words begin with vowels? ☐
    Health and fitness are important to me and my family.
20. Circle the preposition.
    In the future, maybe I will be a professional athlete.

DAY 67

1. Circle the correct spelling. malicious malitious
2. Circle the correct spelling. recieve receive
3. Add the silent letter. de___t
4. Circle the correct spelling. gilty guilty
5. A synonym for *decay* is:
   ☐ dental ☐ rot ☐ deceive
6. In which word are the letters *sub* not a prefix meaning *under*?
   ☐ subway ☐ subtitle ☐ subject
7. The contraction of *should not* is _____ .
8. Circle the correct homophone.
   We *past/passed* the cinema but it was closed.
9. Circle the word with fewer syllables. torrential racial
10. Rewrite each word with *ing* added.
    write _____ begin _____
11. Add one comma.
    For the third time this week Dad's car would not start.
12. Enclose the additional information in commas.
    At the end of the party Dad's 50th we were exhausted.
13. Add commas to the sentence.
    My favourite animals include cats dogs and horses especially ponies.
14. Circle the missing pronoun. I you he she it
    My tooth has broken so .... need to visit the dentist.
15. Circle the missing pronoun. we you they
    Mum will be with me and I know .... will have a long wait.
16. Circle the noun the pronoun refers to.
    Is it true that you broke a tooth once, Pavol?
17. Write the missing pronoun.
    Marco and Leanne, would _____ like to come with us?
18. Add the simple present tense of the verb *to go*.
    Dad _____ to the dentist only if he needs to but I _____ regularly.
19. Add the simple past tense of the verb *to lose*.
    My grandad _____ all his teeth before he was 60.
20. Add the correct part of the verb *to keep*.
    He has _____ his false teeth in a jar, ever since.

DAY 68

1. Circle the correct spelling. nutricious nutritious
2. Circle the correct spelling. field feild
3. Add the silent letter. autum___
4. Circle the correct spelling. sensibley sensibly
5. An antonym for *cruel* is: ☐ crazy ☐ kind
6. Add the suffix *ous* to *glory*. _____
7. *routes* or *roots*? _____
   The tree has a vast system of ....
8. Write a synonym for *purchase*. b_____
9. Listed alphabetically, the third word is _____ .
   flare flimsy flatter flicker
10. Which word does not belong in the group?
    ☐ moth ☐ spider ☐ mosquito ☐ butterfly
11. Circle the speaker and the words spoken.
    The crowd cheered loudly, 'Hurrah for our Olympic champions!'
12. Add punctuation.
    The President joked There's a large crowd here today Is anything special happening
13. Add punctuation.
    Gloria Mallard continued To our dedicated athletes we say congratulations
14. Circle and write the adverb. _____
    Sam watched anxiously as his friend climbed the fence.
15. Circle the prepositions.
    In the dark, he waited for a few minutes behind a big tree.
16. Circle *allowed* or *aloud*.
    'Whose house is this?' Sam wondered
    _____ .
17. Is the underlined word a pronoun? ☐ yes ☐ no
    'Can you give me any reason why you are here?'
18. Circle and write the abstract noun. _____
    Sam was overcome with fear when he heard it.
19. Is the underlined word an adjective? ☐ yes ☐ no
    Our favourite frisbee flew too high for us to catch.
20. Circle the conjunction.
    If you're telling the truth, I won't need to call the guards.

UNIT 7

MY SCORE

MY SCORE

1. Circle the correct spelling.   suspicious   suspitious
2. Circle the correct spelling.   cieling   ceiling
3. Add the silent letter.   whis___le
4. Circle the correct spelling.   relyable   reliable
5. A synonym for **enemy** is:
   ☐ active   ☐ opposite   ☐ foe
6. In which word are the letters **ex** not a prefix meaning **out of**?
   ☐ exact   ☐ export   ☐ excavate
7. The contraction of **will not** is _____ .
8. Circle the correct homophone.
   My father/farther will help at the school fair.
9. Circle the word with fewer syllables.   substantial facial
10. Rewrite each word with **ing** added.
    drum _____   cycle _____
11. Add one comma.
    By taking the short cut we arrived home much earlier.
12. Enclose the additional information in commas.
    According to Beth the lady next door the post came late.
13. Add commas to the sentence.
    Instruments in the school band are violin guitar flute clarinet and recorder.
14. Circle the missing pronoun.   I   you   he   she   it
    As the bus approached our stop, ... crashed into a truck.
15. Circle the missing pronoun.   we   you   they
    The passengers were not injured but .... were shaken.
16. Circle the noun the pronoun refers to.
    The bus could be driven but another arrived to replace it.
17. Write the missing pronoun.
    _____ were late for school but Sue and I had a good excuse!
18. Add the present tense of the verb **to know**.
    The passengers _____ that the driver was not at fault.
19. Add the past tense of the verb **to feel**.
    They all _____ that he did his best to protect them.
20. Add the correct part of the verb **to travel**.
    _____ on public transport is still the best option.

1. Circle the correct spelling.   ficticious   fictitious
2. Circle the correct spelling.   preduce   produce
3. Add the silent letter.   ___nife
4. Circle the correct spelling.   visibley   visibly
5. An antonym for **gloomy** is: ☐ grey   ☐ bright
6. Add the suffix **ial** to **ceremony**. _____
7. **prophecy** or **prophet**? _____
   The evil wizard thought the .... was about him.
8. Write an antonym for **private**.   p_____
9. Listed alphabetically, the first word is _____ .
   gravity   grammar   gradual   graphic
10. Which word does not belong in the group?
    ☐ flower   ☐ leaves   ☐ soil   ☐ stem
11. Circle the speaker and the words spoken.
    Mrs Abbott screamed, 'A mouse! It's a mouse!'
12. Add punctuation.
    Tim from my class spoke calmly Are you afraid of mice Mrs Abbott
13. Add punctuation.
    Mrs Abbott replied nervously No Tim but I didn't expect to find one in my handbag
14. Circle the conjunction.
    Although a little nervous, Eva was now ready to play.
15. Circle the adverb.
    She waited silently in the wings for her turn on stage.
16. Write **peace** or **piece**.
    Each competitor played a _____ of music from memory.
17. Is the underlined word a verb?   ☐ yes   ☐ no
    To calm <u>herself</u>*, Eva closed her eyes as she played.*
18. Circle and write the abstract noun. _____
    When she finished, Eva was overcome with emotion.
19. Circle the verb group.
    Her grandfather's flute had played its magic for Eva.
20. Circle the preposition.
    Her performance earned Eva a place in the youth orchestra.

MY SCORE

MY SCORE

UNIT 7

DAY 71

1. Circle the correct spelling.　　appreciate　　aprecciate

2. Circle the incorrect spelling.　　harras　　harass

3. Circle the incorrect spelling.　　perchase　　purchase

4. Circle the correct spelling.　　imageine　　imagine

5. A synonym for **debate** is:
   ☐ agree　　☐ argue　　☐ fight

6. Circle the correct prefix for the verb.

   As the fog lifted, the distant hills <u>dis/re</u> appeared.

7. Contract.　　who will _____

8. Circle the correct homophone.

   Our hotel <u>suite/sweet</u> at Disneyland was amazing.

9. Count the syllables.

   mischief ☐　　　　opportunity ☐

10. Write the simple present tense verb for **he**, **she** and **it**.

    hurry _____　　study _____

11. Punctuate.

    lots of people enjoy takeaway meals but my family and i prefer home-cooked food

12. Punctuate.

    The summer Olympics have been held in london beijing athens and sydney

13. Which is needed?　☐ a comma　☐ a full stop

    The match is due to start at 3 o'clock ☐ The visiting team has not arrived yet.

14. Circle the words that refer to his notebook.

    Tony lost his notebook: the one with the ripped cover.

15. Circle the phrase the pronoun **them** refers to.

    All his notes were in that book; he felt lost without them.

16. Circle and write the adjective. _____
    The notebook was found in a muddy puddle.

17. Circle and write the verb. _____
    Tony dropped the book on his way home from school.

18. Add the past tense of **to throw**.

    Yesterday, the boys _____ their bags around.

19. Add the present tense of **to know**.

    Do you think he _____ where his book is?

20. Write **advice** or **advise**.

    My _____ would be to look around the school.

DAY 72

1. Circle the incorrect spelling. discrace　　disgrace

2. Circle the correct spelling.　　cushern　　cushion

3. Circle the correct spelling.　　mischievous　　mischevious

4. Circle the incorrect spelling. ancshus　　anxious

5. An antonym for **chaos** is:
   ☐ havoc　　☐ peace　　☐ wonder

6. Add the suffix **ise** to change the noun to a verb.

   atom _____　　cannibal _____

7. **pair** or **pare**? _____

   I need to .... my pencil.

8. Write an antonym for **failure**.　s_____

9. Listed alphabetically, the first word is _____ .

   mummify　　multitude　　mumble　　mumps

10. Which word does not belong in the group?
    ☐ ash　　☐ lava　　☐ magma　　☐ water

11. Add commas.

    The medicine box contained bandages antiseptic cream painkillers and a pair of scissors.

12. The word **ravenous** means:
    ☐ extremely hungry　　☐ a type of bird

13. Punctuate.

    the poster advertised that the circus was coming to new ross

14. Circle the pronoun linked to the noun **mistakes**.

    When we make <u>mistakes</u> we think we have failed, but we can learn a lot from them.

15. Circle the words linked to the pronoun **those**.

    My dad's best meals have been <u>those</u> he cooked after reading the recipes incorrectly.

16. Circle the indefinite article.

    Dad told us to choose a meal for him to cook.

17. Write **choose** or **chose**.

    Which should we _____?

18. Circle the word that makes the meaning of the adjective stronger.

    The meal Dad prepared was absolutely delicious.

19. **Quite** intensifies the adjective _____ .

    Unfortunately, the mess in the kitchen was quite dreadful.

20. Circle and write the conjunction. _____

    The meal was devoured in less than half an hour but the clearing up took much longer.

MY SCORE

MY SCORE

UNIT 8

1. Circle the correct spelling.   autergraph   autograph
2. Circle the incorrect spelling.   frekwently   frequently
3. Circle the correct spelling.   parlament   parliament
4. Circle the incorrect spelling.   tongue   tungue
5. A synonym for **soar** is: ☐ float ☐ land ☐ rise
6. Circle the correct prefix for the verb.

    The hotel had <u>over/under</u> booked and we had nowhere to stay.
7. Contract.   why had _____
8. Circle the correct homophone.

    After the <u>missed/mist</u> cleared, the weather was perfect.
9. Count the syllables.

    accommodate ☐   frequently ☐
10. Write the simple present tense verb for **he**, **she** and **it**.

    marry _____   supply _____

    buy _____
11. Punctuate.

    The river liffey looked like it was going to burst its banks.
12. Add an apostrophe.

    The teachers cars were all in the staff car park.
13. Which is needed? ☐ a comma ☐ a full stop

    Although John agreed to sing in the choir ☐ he was still nervous about it.
14. Circle the word that refers to **chocolates**.

    I bought some <u>chocolates</u> for my mum; she likes any with soft centres.
15. Circle the words that refer to **gift**.

    I wrapped the box of chocolates in paper and placed the <u>gift</u> on the table.
16. Circle and write the verb. _____

    My dad eyed the box with great interest.
17. Circle and write the definite article. _____

    Dad watched the box.
18. Write the correct part of the verb **to jump**.

    Suddenly, Dad _____ out of his chair.
19. Circle the two prepositions.

    Hiding the box behind his back, Dad went into the garden.
20. Circle the expression.

    With a stomach full of chocolates, Dad slept like a baby.

1. Circle the incorrect spelling.   monssoon   monsoon
2. Circle the correct spelling.   recommend   reccomend
3. Circle the incorrect spelling.   revolution   revelootion
4. Circle the correct spelling.   imergency   emergency
5. An antonym for **absurd** is:

    ☐ certain   ☐ insane   ☐ sensible
6. Add the suffix **en** to change the noun to a verb.

    threat _____   fright _____
7. **pair** or **pare** or **pear**? _____

    Do you know where my new .... of socks are?
8. The word **donation** comes from the Latin word **donum** meaning ☐ book ☐ gift
9. Listed alphabetically, the third word is _____.

    podium   poetry   pocket   poem
10. Which word does not belong in the group?

    ☐ Ganymede ☐ Neptune ☐ Saturn
    ☐ Uranus
11. Add commas.

    The indoor activities included basket weaving painting kite making calligraphy and scrapbooking.
12. The word **monotonous** means:

    ☐ dull, boring and unchanging.
    ☐ large, important and outstanding.
13. Circle the verb.

    You have a simple choice: sprouts or peas.
14. Circle the pronoun linked to the underlined words.

    I enjoy <u>long walks in the country</u>; they make me feel very happy and relaxed.
15. Circle the words linked to the pronoun **them**.

    Last time, I wore my new walking boots; my feet felt like they were being massaged by <u>them</u>.
16. Write the correct part of the verb **to decide**.

    It is sometimes hard _____ which walk to go on.
17. Circle and write the indefinite article. _____

    It is time to make a decision.
18. Circle the word that makes the meaning of the adjective stronger.

    The mountain scenery is incredibly beautiful.
19. **Completely** intensifies the phrase _____.

    After a long walk, I am completely worn out.
20. Circle and write the conjunction. _____

    When I walk, I usually think about what's happening in my life at the moment.

MY SCORE

MY SCORE

UNIT 8

1. Circle the correct spelling.   convenience   konvienence
2. Circle the correct spelling.   desgription   description
3. Circle the incorrect spelling.   beautiful   baeutiful
4. Circle the incorrect spelling.   hansome   handsome
5. A synonym for **exhibit** is:
   ☐ conceal   ☐ display   ☐ hide
6. Circle the correct prefix for the verb.
   I mis/un heard the question and wrote the wrong answer.
7. Contract.   where have _____
8. Circle the correct homophone.
   The dentist scares his patience/patients.
9. Count the syllables.
   evaporation ☐   privilege ☐
10. Write the simple present tense verb for **he**, **she** and **it**.
    scurry _____   rely _____
11. Punctuate.
    I hope were not given too much homework tonight
12. Add commas.
    The cruise included stops in Greece Crete Cyprus and Italy.
13. Which is needed? ☐ a comma ☐ a full stop
    If we don't visit Gran today ☐ we won't see her until we return home from holiday.
14. Circle the word that refers to **presentation**.
    We planned our presentation on the computer; Mr Cliff was pleased with our work.
15. Circle the word that **modern technology** refers to.
    Using a computer is really cool; modern technology makes schoolwork lots of fun.
16. Circle and write the verb. _____
    My group gave a PowerPoint™ presentation to the class.
17. Circle the pronoun.
    The class gave a round of applause when we finished.
18. Write the correct part of the verb **to give**.
    We _____ _____ the same presentation at assembly tomorrow.
19. Circle the two prepositions.
    We placed the computer beneath the table and unplugged it from the socket.
20. Circle and write the conjunction. _____
    It was over, so I left the stage in a hurry.

1. Circle the incorrect spelling.   resgue   rescue
2. Circle the incorrect spelling.   deleete   delete
3. Circle the correct spelling.   weather   weathir
4. Circle the correct spelling.   aweful   awful
5. An antonym for **perish** is:
   ☐ crumble   ☐ destroy   ☐ revive
6. Add the suffix **ate** to change the noun to a verb.
   assassin _____
   hyphen _____
7. **during** or **while**? _____
   Mum read her book .... Dad prepared dinner.
8. The word **hostile** comes from the Latin word **hostis** meaning ☐ table ☐ enemy
9. Listed alphabetically, the last word is _____.
   geology   genius   geocentric   gentle
10. Which word does not belong in the group?
    ☐ Algeria ☐ Ethiopia ☐ Libya ☐ Japan
11. Add commas.
    We visited the supermarket two clothes shops a games shop and a bookshop.
12. The word **astrologist** means:
    ☐ a person who studies rock and fossils.
    ☐ a person who studies the stars.
13. Add an apostrophe.
    The ladies scarves were hanging beside their coats.
14. Circle the pronoun linked to the underlined words.
    Next season, we would be in a lower division; we were not looking forward to it.
15. Circle the words linked to the pronoun **it**.
    Our defeat in the match was a complete disaster; it was so embarrassing!
16. Tick. ☐ statement ☐ command
    I don't know what sport to do to keep fit.
17. Circle the error.
    What would you do.
18. Circle the word that makes the meaning of the adjective stronger.
    I want to be really fit when the season starts next year.
19. **So** intensifies the adverb _____.
    I lose my fitness so quickly when I don't exercise.
20. Circle and write the conjunction. _____
    Before I start my off-season training, I will have a rest.

UNIT 8

MY SCORE   MY SCORE

1. Circle the incorrect spelling. answer   arnser
2. Circle the correct spelling.   foorgiveable   forgivable
3. Circle the correct spelling.   jewelery   jewellery
4. Circle the incorrect spelling. feirce   fierce
5. A synonym for **solitary** is:
   ☐ friendly   ☐ isolated   ☐ angry
6. Circle the correct prefix for the verb.
   The rugby referee dis/mis allowed the try.
7. Contract. how would _____
8. Circle the correct homophone.
   My brother was fined/find for driving his car too fast.
9. Count the syllables.
   favourite ☐   explanation ☐
10. Write the simple present tense verb for **he**, **she** and **it**.
    worry _____   bury _____
    say _____
11. Punctuate.
    i still cant believe that our team won.
12. Add commas.
    The zoo housed lions penguins kangaroos snakes seals and giraffes.
13. Add speech marks.
    Michelle announced, I have worked well in school and my results are great.
14. The expression **to smell a rat** means:
    ☐ to smell a very unpleasant odour.
    ☐ to be suspicious.
15. The expression **to take forty winks** means:
    ☐ to sleep.
    ☐ to get dust out of your eye.
16. Circle the adverb.
    The singing birds wake us up early in the mornings.
17. Circle the verbs.
    Dad makes breakfast while Mum drinks tea.
18. Write the correct part of the verb **to go**.
    Dad and I _____ fishing very early this morning.
19. Circle the two prepositions.
    We sat on the river bank and waited in silence.
20. Circle the adjective.
    After a while, Dad caught a huge trout.

1. Circle the correct spelling.   tornado   tornadoe
2. Circle the incorrect spelling. gaurantee   guarantee
3. Circle the incorrect spelling. puase   pause
4. Circle the correct spelling.   lifestyle   lifstyle
5. An antonym for **criticise** is:
   ☐ agree   ☐ blame   ☐ praise
6. Add the suffix **ify** to change the noun to a verb.
   acid _____   solid _____
7. **wandered** or **wondered**? _____
   Amy .... what had happened to her cat.
8. The word **summit** comes from the Latin word **summus** meaning ☐ highest   ☐ middle
9. Listed alphabetically, the second word is _____ .
   brush   browse   bruise   brute
10. Which word does not belong in the group?
    ☐ crow   ☐ ostrich   ☐ swan   ☐ eagle
11. Add commas.
    Dad tried a number of tools to break the lock: a hammer a saw a drill and even a large stone.
12. The word **geologist** means:
    ☐ a person who studies space.
    ☐ a person who studies rocks.
13. Add speech marks.
    The manager offered, Three nights for the price of two.
14. Circle the pronoun linked to the underlined words.
    The ferry trip to the island always makes me sick; I dread it every time we go there.
15. Circle the words linked to the pronoun **them**.
    My friends can have fun straightaway, but before I can join them, I have to rest for a while.
16. Circle the error.
    I'm not sure what time Ill be ready to join you.
17. Tick. ☐ statement   ☐ question   ☐ command
    What will you be doing later?
18. Circle the word that makes the meaning of the adjective stronger.
    It is so unfair that I get seasick.
19. **Very** intensifies the adjective _____ .
    I feel very weak as I have eaten nothing all day.
20. Circle and write the conjunction. _____
    When my stomach settles down, I will join my friends.

DAY 79

1. Circle the correct spelling.　enviroment　environment

2. Circle the incorrect spelling.　extrodinary　extraordinary

3. Circle the correct spelling.　discipline　dissipline

4. Circle the incorrect spelling.　species　speshes

5. A synonym for **summit** is:
   ☐ boundary　　☐ centre　　☐ peak

6. Circle the correct prefix for the verb.
   Sam couldn't de/un lock his bike so he had to walk.

7. Contract.　what are _____

8. Circle the correct homophone.
   There is always a war/wore going on somewhere.

9. Count the syllables.
   appreciate ☐　　　international ☐

10. Write the simple present tense verb for **he**, **she** and **it**.
    carry _____　　try _____

11. Punctuate.
    the television show was interrupted by a breaking news story.

12. Add speech marks.
    The news reporter announced, We interrupt this programme to bring you some shocking news.

13. Add commas.
    The tournament will involve French German Italian and Russian athletes.

14. The expression **to have a bee in your bonnet** means:
    ☐ to be afraid of getting stung
    ☐ to be obsessed with an idea

15. The expression **to throw in the towel** means:
    ☐ to give up a difficult activity
    ☐ to do the laundry

16. Circle and write the verb. _____
    Many teenagers work at fast food restaurants.

17. Circle the proper noun.
    My dog Marble enjoys takeaway scraps.

18. Write the correct part of the verb **to be**.
    While people _____ eating, Marble waits quietly under the table.

19. Circle the two prepositions.
    Marble eats his dinner from his bowl, which is near the back door.

20. Circle:　present tense　　past tense
    He empties his bowl in a flash.

DAY 80

1. Circle the incorrect spelling.　immediately　immediatly

2. Circle the correct spelling.　graceful　gracefull

3. Circle the incorrect spelling.　grusome　gruesome

4. Circle the correct spelling.　aurthor　author

5. An antonym for **excavate** is:
   ☐ bury　　☐ dig　　☐ scrape

6. Add the suffix **ise** to change the noun to a verb.
   memory _____
   apology _____

7. **stake** or **steak**? _____
   The farmer needs a wooden .... for his fence.

8. Write a synonym for **cure**.　r_____

9. Listed alphabetically, the last word is _____ .
   delicate　　deliberate　　delight　　delicious

10. Which word does not belong in the group?
    ☐ hail　　☐ rain　　☐ snow　　☐ wind

11. Add commas.
    I like reading about unicorns goblins giants centaurs dragons and wizards.

12. The word **biologist** means:
    ☐ a person who studies living things.
    ☐ a person who studies history.

13. Circle the definite article.
    The catalogue said 'More price reductions instore!'

14. Circle the pronoun linked to the underlined words.
    The stolen goods were unique so the police think they have a good chance of tracing them.

15. Circle the words linked to **either one**.
    Two windows had been left open; the thieves could have gained access through either one.

16. Circle the word that is not needed.
    What chance do we have of getting everything back up?

17. Write **your** or **our**.
    What should we do in future to identify _____ things?

18. Circle the word that makes the meaning of the adjective stronger.
    It is most unusual for us to leave any windows open.

19. **Still** intensifies the adjective _____ .
    It is still possible that our things may be found.

20. Circle and write the conjunction. _____
    My guitar was taken but, thankfully, not my flute.

MY SCORE

MY SCORE

DAY 81

1. Circle the correct spelling.   aparent   apparent

2. Circle the incorrect spelling.   schedule   scedule

3. Circle the correct spelling.   sustane   sustain

4. Circle the incorrect spelling.   fued   feud

5. A synonym for **harsh** is:
   ☐ angry   ☐ cruel   ☐ strange

6. Circle the correct prefix for the verb.

   Matt was often told off because of his dis/in ability to sit still.

7. Contract.   who is _____   who has _____

8. Circle the correct homophone.

   Explorers searched for the sauce/source of the River Nile.

9. Count the syllables.   citizen ☐   majority ☐

10. Write the simple past tense for the third person singular.

    buy _____   study _____

11. Punctuate.

    what are you doing asked my best friend

12. Punctuate.

    ouch cried matthew that hurt my arm

13. Punctuate.

    dad likes lettuce tomatoes and onions in his sandwich

14. Add an apostrophe.

    Jacks parents took him to the airport.

15. This sentence is in the _____ tense.

    Jack's luggage was weighed by the man at the check-in desk.

16. A ☐ preposition ☐ conjunction follows the verb group.

    The plane was delayed by bad weather.

17. Circle the reflexive pronoun.

    Jack always enjoyed himself when he travelled alone.

18. Add the reflexive pronoun **himself** or **yourself**.

    He likes restaurants where he can serve

    _____.

19. Circle the conjunctions that work together as a pair.

    Jack's favourite cuisine is either Vietnamese or Italian.

20. Circle the infinitive of the verb.

    The seasoned traveller will be back home to celebrate his birthday.

DAY 82

1. Circle the incorrect spelling.   catergry   category

2. Circle the correct spelling.   voucher   voacher

3. Circle the incorrect spelling.   occurred   ocurred

4. Circle the correct spelling.   amater   amateur

5. An antonym for **reveal** is:
   ☐ cover   ☐ display   ☐ show

6. Add the suffix **ion** or **ation** to change the verb to a noun.

   collect _____   inform _____

7. **stake** or **steak**? _____

   Dad ordered a .... for his meal.

8. The word **magnify** comes from the Latin word **magna** meaning   ☐ large   ☐ leaf

9. Listed alphabetically, the last word is _____.

   cameo   calico   camera   calorie

10. Which word does not belong in the group?
    ☐ canteen   ☐ library   ☐ office   ☐ field

11. Punctuate.

    no he replied i have to go to the park first

12. Punctuate.

    what is the capital of peru julie asked

13. Punctuate.

    laois kilkenny and kildare are all in leinster.

14. Circle the verb group and the preposition.

    Gum disease is caused by plaque.

15. Rewrite the sentence in the correct order.

    bacteria   caused   by   plaque   is

    _____

16. Rewrite the sentence in the correct order.

    brushing   plaque   reduces   regular

    _____

17. Circle the reflexive pronoun.

    Do you watch yourself when you brush your teeth?.

18. Add the correct reflexive pronoun.

    Dad often hurts _____ when he flosses his teeth.

19. Circle the word that connects the two sentences.

    When my granny was young, dental floss was not available; consequently, she has lost most of her teeth.

20. Circle the correct connecting word.   finally   instead

    My last baby tooth refused to fall out; ...., it came out while I was eating dinner.

1. Circle the correct spelling.　conshence　conscience
2. Circle the incorrect spelling.　afterwards　afterwurds
3. Circle the correct spelling.　glacier　glasier
4. Circle the incorrect spelling.　sossidge　sausage
5. A synonym for *tender* is:
   ⬭ gentle　⬭ smooth　⬭ tough
6. Circle the correct prefix for the verb.
   The teacher's in/re action to Eric's trick was not good.
7. Contract.　why are _____　why have _____
8. Circle the correct homophone.
   This pair/pare/pear is not ripe enough to eat.
9. Count the syllables.
   research ⬭　technology ⬭
10. Add the simple past tense for the third person singular.
    hurry _____　supply _____
11. Punctuate.
    j k rowling wrote the harry potter series
12. Punctuate.
    I asked my friend did you get concert tickets
13. Punctuate.
    I like milk chocolate said Ryan, but I don't like white chocolate
14. The sentence is in the _____ tense.
    The author was applauded by the waiting crowd.
15. Circle the verbs.
    Unknown actors portrayed the main characters.
16. A ⬭ preposition ⬭ noun follows the verb group.
    The actors were catapulted to stardom by the film.
17. Circle the reflexive pronoun.
    The author surprised herself by writing such a great story.
18. Add the correct reflexive pronoun.　ourselves　themselves
    After the success of the first book in the series,
    the others sold _____ .
19. Circle the conjunction that works together with the underlined conjunction.
    The author was not only delighted by her success but also surprised.
20. Circle the phrase that refers to the author.
    The award-winning celebrity is already working on her next book.

1. Circle the incorrect spelling.　equippment　equipment
2. Circle the correct spelling.　quarantine　quaranteen
3. Circle the incorrect spelling.　colom　column
4. Circle the correct spelling.　encurage　encourage
5. Circle an antonym for *detest*.　adore　dislike　suffer
6. Add the suffix *ion* or *ation* to change the verb to a noun.
   populate _____　imagine _____
7. *many* or *much*? _____
   I put too .... flour in the cake; it was like a rock.
8. Write a synonym for *annually*.　y_____
9. Listed alphabetically, the last word is _____ .
   defuse　degrade　deflect　degree
10. Circle the word that does not belong in the group.
    badminton　basketball　tennis　volleyball
11. Punctuate.
    the woman yelled close the door after you
12. Punctuate.
    who scored the goal enquired Niamh
13. Punctuate.
    william shakespeare wrote macbeth
14. Circle the verb group and the preposition.
    Obesity is caused by overeating.
15. Rewrite the sentence in the correct order.
    diet　promote　exercise　health　and　good
    _____
16. Rewrite the sentence in the correct order.
    wellbeing a feeling healthy creates lifestyle a of
    _____
17. Circle the reflexive pronoun.
    As we grow, we learn to look after ourselves.
18. Add the correct reflexive pronoun.
    Dedicated athletes motivate _____ to train.
19. Circle the word that connects the two sentences.
    Some people don't seem to care about their health; instead, they eat excessively and do little or no exercise.
20. Which connecting word?　meanwhile　otherwise
    Develop good habits while you are young; .... you will have health problems later in life.

MY SCORE

MY SCORE

UNIT 9

1. Circle the correct spelling. goverment government

2. Circle the incorrect spelling. apolergise apologise

3. Circle the correct spelling. probabel probable

4. Circle the incorrect spelling. effishent efficient

5. A synonym for **sturdy** is:
   ☐ durable   ☐ soft   ☐ straight

6. Circle the correct prefix for the verb.
   I am not dis/un like my sister in character.

7. Contract. how are _____ how have _____

8. Circle the correct homophone.
   The river currant/current is very strong near the bridge.

9. Count the syllables. foreign ☐ surgery ☐

10. Add the simple past tense for the third person singular.
    say _____   rely _____

11. Punctuate.
    The bus driver announced the bus is full.

12. Punctuate.
    johnny depp is an american actor.

13. Punctuate.
    charles dickens wrote a christmas carol.

14. The sentence is in the _____ tense.
    Pollution from a factory destroyed the life in the river.

15. Circle the adverb.
    The company was fined heavily by the local council.

16. A ☐ preposition ☐ conjunction follows the verb group.
    The company was ordered by the local council to repair the damage.

17. Circle the reflexive pronoun.
    A polluted river cannot clean itself.

18. Add the correct reflexive pronoun.
    Company owners should be ashamed of
    _____ *for causing such environmental problems.*

19. Circle the conjunctions that work together as a pair.
    The owners neither know nor care about the environmental problems they are causing.

20. Circle the phrase that refers to the company owners.
    These greedy, selfish people with no principles care nothing for the future of our planet.

1. Circle the incorrect spelling. prejerdice prejudice

2. Circle the correct spelling. definate definite

3. Circle the incorrect spelling. reversible reversable

4. Circle the correct spelling. agenst against

5. An antonym for **captivity** is:
   ☐ freedom   ☐ hostage   ☐ imprisonment

6. Add the suffix **ion** or **ation** to change the verb to a noun.
   reflect _____   confirm _____

7. **site** or **sight**? _____
   The building .... was filled with workers.

8. Write an antonym for **liquid**. s_____

9. Listed alphabetically, the last word is _____.
   finance   fillet   finale   filter

10. Which word does not belong in the group?
    ☐ Ireland ☐ Austria ☐ Malta ☐ Iceland

11. Punctuate.
    there is so much to do complained edel

12. Punctuate.
    denise said your really kind brother will help you

13. Punctuate.
    Claire said id love to help but im going shopping

14. Circle the verb group and the preposition.
    Tourists are delighted by the architecture, language, cuisine and culture of foreign countries.

15. Rewrite the sentence in the correct order.
    appreciate   foods   traditional   tourists
    _____

16. Rewrite the sentence in the correct order.
    local   enjoy   tourists   festivals
    _____

17. Circle the reflexive pronoun.
    Tourists enjoy themselves at local markets.

18. Add the correct reflexive pronoun.
    We should be proud of _____ if we can speak the local language.

19. Circle the word that connects the two sentences.
    People like visitors to their country to try to speak their language; besides, it is good manners to make the effort.

20. Which connecting word? however   similarly
    Practising a new language is fun; ...., if you have no idea, just smile and use sign language!

UNIT 9

MY SCORE

MY SCORE

1. Circle the correct spelling.   fiber   fibre

2. Circle the incorrect spelling.   shreik   shriek

3. Circle the correct spelling.   cerllection collection

4. Circle the incorrect spelling.   frightning   frightening

5. A synonym for *friendly* is:
   ☐ amiable   ☐ happy   ☐ good

6. Circle the correct prefix for the verb.
   I love that book and have mis/re read it many times.

7. Contract.
   when are _____   when have _____

8. Circle the correct homophone.
   The moose/mousse walked into town looking for food.

9. Count the syllables. experiment ☐ measure ☐

10. Add the simple past tense for the third person singular.
    scurry _____   bury _____

    pray _____

11. Punctuate.
    susan murphy the captain of the football team
    encouraged her teammates

12. Punctuate.
    Marie whispered i hid the money in the safe

13. Punctuate.
    Roald dahl wrote the witches

14. The sentence is in the _____ tense.
    Danny always spoiled Mungo.

15. Circle the adverb.
    Danny was loved unconditionally by Mungo.

16. A ☐ preposition ☐ conjunction follows the verb
    group.
    Danny was surprised by the cost of keeping a dog.

17. Circle the reflexive pronoun.
    A dog cannot look after itself; it needs love and care.

18. Add the correct reflexive pronoun.
    When Danny goes to school, Mungo cannot take

    _____ *for a walk.*

19. Circle the conjunctions that work together as a pair.
    Mungo is not a pedigree but a mongrel.

20. Circle the phrase that refers to Mungo.
    Danny cannot imagine life without his faithful, fun-
    loving partner in crime.

MY SCORE

1. Circle the incorrect spelling.   theeater   theatre

2. Circle the correct spelling.   expression   expreshion

3. Circle the incorrect spelling.   review   reveiw

4. Circle the correct spelling.   orgernise   organise

5. An antonym for *humble* is:
   ☐ proud   ☐ sincere   ☐ sly

6. Add the suffix *ion* or *ation* to change the verb to a noun.
   erupt _____   preserve _____

7. *site* or *sighf*? _____
   The .... of the beautiful lake made me happy.

8. Write a synonym for *option*.   c_____

9. Listed alphabetically, the last word is _____ .
   guest   guide   guard   guess

10. Which word does not belong in the group?
    ☐ grizzly   ☐ buffalo   ☐ panda   ☐ polar

11. Punctuate.
    I think those animals are called antelope said Dara

12. Punctuate.
    one of my favourite films is shrek.

13. Punctuate.
    inspector mulligan the leader of the investigation
    caught the culprit

14. Circle the verb group and the preposition.
    Many young people are fascinated by martial arts.

15. Rewrite the sentence in the correct order.
    athletes by affected badly some fame are

    _____

16. Rewrite the sentence in the correct order.
    future successful athletes stars coach

    _____

17. Circle the reflexive pronoun.
    Some athletes punish themselves when they don't
    perform well.

18. Add the correct reflexive pronoun.
    The important thing is for us to enjoy

    _____ .

19. Circle the word that connects the two sentences.
    We can choose the activities we want to do; also, we can
    decide how serious we will be about them.

20. Circle the correct connecting word.   indeed   then
    We can make a list of possible activities; .... we can
    plan when and where to do them.

MY SCORE

UNIT 9

1. Circle the correct spelling. accomerdat accommodate
2. Circle the incorrect spelling. disgussion discussion
3. Circle the correct spelling. except exsept
4. Circle the incorrect spelling. perspone postpone
5. A synonym for **grateful** is:
   ☐ free ☐ kind ☐ thankful
6. Circle the correct prefix for the verb.
   The electrician dis/re connected the power before starting work.
7. Contract. what are _____ what have _____
8. Circle the correct homophone.
   The evil king's reign/rein was short-lived.
9. Count the syllables.
   ecosystem ☐   conclusion ☐
10. Add the simple past tense for the third person singular.
    worry _____   try _____
    play _____
11. Punctuate.
    bronagh peter ian bill and katie were not in school today.
12. Punctuate.
    were they all sick I asked
13. Punctuate.
    I love the song silent night
14. Circle the verb group.
    The information technology industry has made some people very wealthy.
15. The sentence is in the _____ tense.
    Dad's phone was washed in the machine by Mum.
16. A ☐ preposition ☐ conjunction follows the verb group.
    This wasn't the first time an expensive item was washed by Mum in this way.
17. Circle the reflexive pronoun.
    Mum laughed and said, 'Don't upset yourself, dear!'
18. Add the correct reflexive pronoun.
    Dad had to try and calm _____ down!
19. Circle the conjunctions that work together as a pair.
    Dad was both angry and amused by Mum's reaction.
20. Circle the phrase that refers to Mum's sense of humour.
    Dad loves the spirited, fun-loving demon that makes Mum such fun to be with.

1. Circle the incorrect spelling. committee cermittee
2. Circle the correct spelling. permishion permission
3. Circle the incorrect spelling. hyumour humour
4. Circle the correct spelling. dignerty dignity
5. An antonym for **noble** is:
   ☐ brave ☐ dishonourable ☐ loyal
6. Add the suffix **ion** or **ation** to change the verb to a noun.
   express _____   conserve _____
7. **peace** or **piece**? _____
   Would you like a .... of lemon pie?
8. The word **spectator** comes from the Latin word **spectare** meaning ☐ jump ☐ to watch
9. Listed alphabetically, the last word is _____ .
   laundry   laugh   laurel   launch
10. Which word does not belong in the group?
    ☐ lake ☐ ocean ☐ river ☐ stream
11. Punctuate.
    do not run across the road warned mum
12. Punctuate.
    I would never do that mum replied frank.
13. Punctuate.
    eoin colfer wrote the book artemis fowl
14. Circle the verb group and the preposition.
    Recent immigrants to the country are helped by free English conversation classes.
15. Rewrite the sentence in the correct order.
    selection libraries a great books have of
    _____
16. Rewrite the sentence in the correct order.
    story children time enjoy young
    _____
17. Circle the reflexive pronoun.
    I can 'lose myself' in a library.
18. Add the correct reflexive pronoun.
    My sister imagines _____ as a librarian.
19. Circle the word that connects the two sentences.
    The opening hours of the local library have been extended because it is so popular.
20. Which connecting word? meanwhile next
    I spend my time looking for interesting novels to read; ...., Mum is lost in the travel section.

1. Circle the correct spelling.   approval   aproval

2. Circle the incorrect spelling.   voluntry   voluntary

3. Circle the correct spelling.   electrishan   electrician

4. Circle the incorrect spelling.   suspend   serspend

5. A synonym for *arrange* is:
   ☐ organise   ☐ put   ☐ add

6. Circle the correct prefix for the word.
   A *bi/tri* cycle has two wheels.

7. Expand.   would've _____

8. Circle the correct homophone.
   The *plain/plane* soared over the mountains.

9. Count the syllables.
   deciduous ☐   coniferous ☐

10. Write the past and present participles of the verb *betray*.
    was _____   is _____

11. Which sentence means that more people know Anna than any other player?
    ☐ Anna is the <u>best-known</u> player on the team.
    ☐ Anna is the <u>best known</u> player on the team.

12. Add speech marks to show direct speech.
    Help me! cried Jay. I think I'm falling!

13. Punctuate.
    Wheres the dogs blanket asked Mum

14. Add the correct pronoun.   I   me   mine   myself
    That is your drink and this one is _____ .

15. Add the correct pronoun.   he   him   his   himself
    When I last saw _____ , Dad was in the shed.

16. Circle the adverb.
    Kay usually arrived home between four and five o'clock.

17. Circle the proper noun.
    The short but steep walk gave Kay no time to think.

18. Circle the nouns.
    The bird sitting on the wall watched Kay closely.

19. The underlined text is: ☐ the infinitive of a verb.
                               ☐ a phrase.
    It did not want Kay <u>to discover</u> where its nest was.

20. Circle the conjunction.
    Kay did not notice the bird so its nest was safe.

1. Circle the incorrect spelling.   telervision   television

2. Circle the correct spelling.   contentment   contentmant

3. Circle the incorrect spelling.   drought   drowt

4. Circle the correct spelling.   transbort   transport

5. An antonym for *repel* is:
   ☐ disgust   ☐ reject   ☐ attract

6. Change each verb to a noun ending in *ion*.
   extend _____   confuse _____

7. *pain* or *pane*? _____
   Please don't let the ball hit the window ....

8. The word *construct* comes from the Latin word
   construere meaning   ☐ to build   ☐ walk

9. Listed alphabetically, the first word is _____ .
   antiseptic   antler   antidote   antique

10. Circle the two words that are part of the same word family.
    familiar   family   famine

11. Add the apostrophe.
    Jim and Joes party was held on Saturday.

12. Add apostrophes.
    The vet treated Pippas and Kates ponies.

13. Add the *apostrophe(s)* and the *letter s*.
    Emma___ and Sam___ mums were both there.

14. Add the correct pronoun.
    anyone   everyone   no-one
    I can't see _____ at the door.

15. Add the correct pronoun.
    Who   Whom   Whose   What   Which
    _____ of these films shall we watch next?

16. Circle the correct word.
    Mum works the (harder/hardest) in the hospital.

17. Circle the word that intensifies *rewarding*.
    She finds her work extremely rewarding.

18. Circle the indefinite article.
    Today, Mum tended a young boy choking on a bone.

19. The underlined text is: ☐ the infinitive of a verb.
                               ☐ a phrase.
    The boy had been taken <u>to the hospital</u> in an ambulance.

20. Circle the feminine noun.
    The tigress protected her cubs.

UNIT 10

MY SCORE

MY SCORE

1. Circle the correct spelling.   ortopsy   autopsy
2. Circle the incorrect spelling.   ciclist   cyclist
3. Circle the correct spelling.   literassy   literacy
4. Circle the incorrect spelling.   prepear   prepare
5. A synonym for **analyse** is:
   ☐ write   ☐ read   ☐ understand
6. Circle the correct prefix for the word.
   You can talk over long distances by micro/tele phone.
7. Expand.   could've _____
8. Circle the correct homophone.
   Is the right/write side of a ship port or starboard?
9. Count the syllables.   physician ☐   politician ☐
10. Write the past and present participles of the verb **bully**.
    was _____   is _____
11. Match the underlined words to their meaning.
    Ⓐ *Bill prefers free range eggs.*
    Ⓑ *Bill prefers free-range eggs.*
    ☐ Bill prefers eggs that cost nothing.
    ☐ Bill prefers eggs laid by free-roaming hens.
12. Add speech marks to show direct speech.
    Walking into the kitchen, Joe asked, What's cooking?
13. Punctuate.
    Are the girls toys inside their bags asked the mans wife
14. Add the correct pronoun.   you   yours   yourself
    Did you hurt _____ when you fell over?
15. Add the correct pronoun.
    they   theirs   themselves
    My friends taught _____ how to play chess.
16. Circle the adverb.
    Kane wandered aimlessly down the hillside.
17. Circle the preposition.
    The crimson evening sun blazed across the valley.
18. Circle the nouns.
    The long shadows created by the sun made interesting patterns on the land.
19. The underlined text is: ☐ the infinitive of a verb.
                                ☐ a phrase.
    Kane felt the sun on his back as he walked to his destination.
20. Circle the conjunction.
    Although he was tired, Kane kept walking.

1. Circle the incorrect spelling.   factory   factry
2. Circle the correct spelling.   cownter   counter
3. Circle the incorrect spelling.   recent   rescent
4. Circle the correct spelling.   examination   examernation
5. An antonym for **obey** is:
   ☐ deny   ☐ ignore   ☐ follow
6. Change each verb to a noun ending in **ion**.
   attend _____   reduce _____
7. **calendar** or **colander**? _____
   I used the .... to drain the pasta.
8. Write an antonym for **guilty**.   i_____
9. Listed alphabetically, the second word is _____.
   charade   charisma   charcoal   charity
10. Circle the two words that are part of the same word family.
    courteous   courtesy   courtyard
11. Add the apostrophe.
    Troy and Taryns parents are international celebrities.
12. Add apostrophes.
    Rexs and Rovers tails were wagging enthusiastically.
13. Add the **apostrophe(s)** and the **letter s** if needed.
    Brian___ and Bill___ house was damaged in the storm.
14. Add the correct pronoun.   who   whom   that
    Cats _____ roam at night can cause trouble.
15. Add the correct pronoun.   this   these   those
    I must finish _____ book before I begin the next one.
16. Circle the correct word.
    Who is taller/tallest, John or Joe?
17. Circle the word that intensifies **annoyed**.
    My little brother gets really annoyed when he loses.
18. Circle the masculine noun.
    My aunt gave her nephew a new bike.
19. The underlined text is: ☐ the infinitive of a verb.
                                ☐ a phrase.
    Jim needs to learn that losing is not the end of the world.
20. Circle the nouns that have common gender.
    A nurse and a teacher attended the meeting.

MY SCORE   MY SCORE

UNIT 10

1. Circle the correct spelling.   publication   publercation
2. Circle the incorrect spelling.   sheild   shield
3. Circle the correct spelling.   fergiveness   forgiveness
4. Circle the incorrect spelling.   shaken   shakern
5. A synonym for **decide** is:
   ☐ choose   ☐ decipher   ☐ declare
6. Circle the correct prefix for the verb.
   To brighten the room, we re/un painted the walls.
7. Expand.   should've _____
8. Circle the correct homophone.
   The ship had a steal/steel hull.
9. Count the syllables.   percussion ☐   mission ☐
10. Write the past and present participles of the verb **decay**.
    was _____   is _____
11. Match the underlined words to their meaning.
    Ⓐ *The bank gave the shop a small-business grant.*
    Ⓑ *The bank gave the shop a small business grant.*
    ☐ The grant was a small amount of money.
    ☐ Only small businesses are entitled to these grants.
12. Add speech marks to show direct speech.
    What a great song! marvelled Ali. Who's singing?
13. Punctuate.
    Whatve you done to it asked the childs big sister
14. Add the correct pronoun.   we   us   ours   ourselves
    We finished the work _____ .
15. Add the correct pronoun.   this   that   these   those
    Those cakes are delicious, but have you tried
    _____?
16. Circle the adverb.
    Tara almost fell off her bike on her way to school.
17. Circle the verb group.
    Tara was shaken after her scare.
18. Circle the definite article.
    The girl who has never fallen off her bike has kept her record.
19. The underlined text is: ☐ the infinitive of a verb.
                                ☐ a phrase.
    Tara wants to compete in bike races when she is older.
20. Circle the conjunctions.
    For relaxation, Tara either reads or plays computer games.

1. Circle the incorrect spelling.   diserbedient   disobedient
2. Circle the correct spelling.   discusting   disgusting
3. Circle the incorrect spelling.   unbalanced   unbalernced
4. Circle the correct spelling.   rasberry   raspberry
5. An antonym for **perish** is:
   ☐ destroy   ☐ survive   ☐ work
6. Change each verb to a noun ending in **ion**.
   corrode _____   infuse _____
7. **pain** or **pane**? _____
   I had a .... in my arm when the ball hit me.
8. Write a synonym for **stop**.   h_____
9. Listed alphabetically, the second word is _____ .
   culture   culminate   cultivate   culprit
10. Circle the two words that are part of the same word family.
    enter   entrance   entreat
11. Add the apostrophe.
    Tim cleaned the filter of Goldies tank.
12. Add apostrophes.
    Tiana collected Bellas and Zenas feathers from their cage.
13. Add an apostrophe.
    Susan collected Pollys feathers that were in the cage.
14. The correct pronoun is: ☐ anybody   ☐ everybody
                                ☐ nobody   ☐ somebody
    There must be .... who can solve the problem.
15. Add the correct pronoun.   who   whom   which
    You will be rewarded for your work, _____ has improved.
16. Circle the correct word.
    Who is the (taller, tallest)—John, Joe or Jack?
17. Circle the word that intensifies **windy**.
    If it is too windy, we won't be able to fly our small kites.
18. Circle the nouns.
    Small kites need a wind that won't break their frames.
19. The underlined text is: ☐ the infinitive of a verb.
                                ☐ a phrase.
    We sometimes go to the beach to fly our kites.
20. Circle the nouns that have common gender.
    My sister and her friend gave directions to the tourist.

UNIT 10

MY SCORE

MY SCORE

DAY 97

1. Circle the correct spelling. circumfrence circumference
2. Circle the incorrect spelling. depression derpression
3. Circle the correct spelling. decision descision
4. Circle the incorrect spelling. rellation relation
5. A synonym for **boast** is:
   ☐ bully ☐ brag ☐ shout
6. Circle the correct prefix for the verb.
   After the race, the jockey dis/re mounted his horse.
7. Expand. might've _____
8. Circle the correct homophone.
   The beach/beech is a deciduous tree.
9. Count the syllables. direction ☐ proportion ☐
10. Write the past and present participles of the verb **destroy**.
    was _____ is _____
11. Match the underlined words to their meaning.
    Ⓐ *The ill-clothed baby lay in the pram.*
    Ⓑ *The ill clothed baby lay in the pram.*
    ☐ The baby was ill and clothed.
    ☐ The baby was badly clothed but not ill.
12. Add speech marks to show direct speech.
    Who else is coming? asked Mum. I need to know.
13. Punctuate.
    Whod have thought to look there cried Li in surprise
14. Add the correct pronoun. it itself
    The car locked _____ with the keys inside.
15. Add the correct pronoun.
    Who Whom Whose What Which
    To find the owner, the teacher asked, '_____ is it?'
16. Circle the adverb.
    Dad sat on the sofa and immediately fell asleep.
17. Circle the definite article.
    His deep rumbling snores could be heard in the garden.
18. Circle the nouns.
    The cat lying by the fire got up, stretched and left the room.
19. The underlined text is: ☐ the infinitive of a verb.
    ☐ a phrase.
    The disgruntled cat returned to its basket.
20. Circle the conjunction.
    The cat returned to the fireside when Dad finally woke up.

DAY 98

1. Circle the incorrect spelling. merchinery machinery
2. Circle the correct spelling. bilingwal bilingual
3. Circle the incorrect spelling. primary primery
4. Circle the correct spelling. doubtful doutful
5. An antonym for **disperse** is:
   ☐ scatter ☐ collect ☐ leave
6. Change each verb to a noun ending in **ion**.
   exclude _____ collide _____
7. **Its** or **It's**? _____
   .... hard to concentrate if you have a pain.
8. Write an antonym for **junior**. s_____
9. Listed alphabetically, the third word is _____.
   fete fettuccine fetlock fetch
10. Circle the two words that are part of the same word family.
    flour flourish floury
11. Add the apostrophe.
    Harry tidied Mum and Dads office for extra pocket money.
12. Add apostrophes.
    Harry also washed Grandmas and Grandpas cars.
13. Add the **apostrophe(s)** and the **letter s** if needed.
    Uncle Ed___ and Aunt Bea___ lawn was another task.
14. Add the correct pronoun. who whom which that
    People _____ exercise regularly feel better.
15. Add the correct pronoun. this that these those
    How did _____ book get over here?
16. Circle the correct word.
    Which is the (better, best) one—my book or yours?
17. Circle the word that intensifies **relieved**.
    He was so relieved to have moved it off the road.
18. Circle the masculine noun.
    It was caused by a ram running into the road.
19. The underlined text is: ☐ the infinitive of a verb.
    ☐ a phrase.
    He tried to call for help but there was no phone reception.
20. Circle the nouns that have common gender.
    The parent waited outside while the pupil was singing.

MY SCORE

MY SCORE

1. Circle the correct spelling.   disgovery   discovery
2. Circle the incorrect spelling.   packidge   package
3. Circle the correct spelling.   derlighted   delighted
4. Circle the incorrect spelling.   reaxtion   reaction
5. A synonym for **startle** is:
   ☐ surprise   ☐ terrify   ☐ speed
6. Circle the correct prefix for the verb.
   The removalists re/un loaded the van's contents.
7. Expand.   must've _____
8. Circle the correct homophone.
   A lot of household waist/waste could be recycled.
9. Count the syllables.
   demonstration ☐   competition ☐
10. Write the past and present participles of the verb **occupy**.
    was _____   is _____
11. Match the underlined words to their meaning.
    (A) *The little-used instrument was for sale.*
    (B) *The little used instrument was for sale.*
    ☐ The instrument was small and had been used.
    ☐ The instrument had hardly been used.
12. Add speech marks to show direct speech.
    As the opposition scored again, Dad cried, Oh no!
13. Punctuate.
    That dogs taken my sausages shouted Dad angrily
14. Add the correct pronoun.   she   her   hers   herself
    Gina knew the designs were _____ .
15. Add the correct pronoun.   this   that   these   those
    'None of _____ for me!' cried Amy, seeing the cabbage.
16. Circle the adverb.
    Mum usually buys cakes if she shops at night.
17. Circle.   present tense   past tense
    She cannot resist the naughty but nice bakery aisle.
18. Circle the nouns.
    The man working at the checkout noticed the contents of Mum's basket.
19. The underlined text is: ☐ the infinitive of a verb.
                         ☐ a phrase.
    Walking to her car, Mum decided to buy fewer cakes in future.
20. Circle the conjunction.
    The cakes were decadent but delicious.

1. Circle the incorrect spelling.   passenger   passinger
2. Circle the correct spelling.   assistance   assistence
3. Circle the incorrect spelling.   desend   descend
4. Circle the correct spelling.   heroic   herroic
5. An antonym for **donate** is:
   ☐ give   ☐ receive   ☐ take
6. Change each verb to a noun ending in **ion**.
   translate _____   divide _____
7. **export** or **import**? _____
   We .... goods into our country.
8. Write a synonym for **inside**.   i_____
9. Listed alphabetically, the last word is _____ .
   girder   gingham   gild   ginger
10. Circle the two words that are part of the same word family.
    creation   crease   creative
11. Add the apostrophe.
    Cher and Dollys duets were a great success.
12. Add apostrophes.
    Chers and Dollys music careers began long ago.
13. Add the **apostrophe(s)** and the **letter s** if needed.
    Cher___ and Dolly___ homes are far apart.
14. Add the correct pronoun.
    Anything   Everything   Nothing   Something
    _____ must be in place from the beginning.
15. Add the correct pronoun.   who   whom   which   that
    People _____ work hard are rewarded.
16. Circle the correct word.
    The old man was the (wiser, wisest) of them all.
17. Circle the word that intensifies **relieved**.
    The crew were very relieved to have crossed the line first.
18. Circle the nouns.
    They threw their captain into the river!
19. The underlined text is: ☐ the infinitive of a verb.
                         ☐ a phrase.
    The captain found it difficult to swim.
20. Circle the nouns that have common gender.
    The widow gave a lift to an adult and a child.

UNIT 10

MY SCORE

MY SCORE

1. Circle the correct spelling.   disgover   discover
2. Circle the incorrect spelling.   hopeful   hopefull
3. Circle the correct spelling.   comfortable   confortable
4. Circle the incorrect spelling.   cinerma   cinema
5. A synonym for **umpire** is:
   ☐ coach   ☐ referee   ☐ player
6. Rearrange the letters to spell the opposite of **public**.
   riptave _____
7. Write the plural.
   child _____   goose _____
8. Circle the correct homophone.
   The mail/male seahorse, not the female, incubates the eggs.
9. Count the syllables.   furthermore ☐   whereas ☐
10. Write the past and present participles of the verb **beg**.
    past _____   present _____
11. Who is speaking? _____
    Entering the room, Rita cried, 'Oh good, they're all in here!'
12. Add commas.
    Rita sat down coughed and quietly said 'So who will help me?'
13. Punctuate.
    Rita wanted to sow seeds in her neighbours garden but she couldn't do it all by herself.
14. Circle and write the plural noun. _____
    Some countries in the world have spectacular scenery.
15. Circle the word that means **a beautiful view**.
    Mountainous regions are particularly scenic.
16. Circle the expression that means a **depressing person**.
    a chip off the old block   a wet blanket
17. Circle the correct verb.
    The wild dogs attack/attacks the carcass.
18. Circle and write the abstract noun. _____
    To the climbers' relief, the fog lifted and the path reappeared.
19. This word is a: ☐ noun   ☐ pronoun.
    The climbers managed to haul themselves over the final obstacle.
20. Circle and write the verb. _____
    The relieved climbers arrived home extremely late.

1. Circle the incorrect spelling.   accerdent   accident
2. Circle the correct spelling.   family   famerly
3. Circle the incorrect spelling.   lotion   loshern
4. Circle the correct spelling.   translate   tranzlate
5. An antonym for **frequently** is:
   ☐ always   ☐ often   ☐ seldom
6. Change each noun to an adjective ending in **ive**.
   comprehension   _____
   exhaustion   _____
7. **check** or **cheque**?   _____
   Mum wrote a .... to pay for the sofa.
8. Write an antonym of **inferior**.   s_____
9. Listed alphabetically, the first word is _____ .
   weather   weary   weave   weak
10. Circle the word that does not belong in the word family.
    carnivorous   devour   voracious   voucher
11. Add the apostrophe.
    Sean and Pats dogs needed a long walk.
12. Add apostrophes.
    Seans and Pats jackets were soaked after the walk.
13. Add the **apostrophe(s)** and the **letter s** if needed.
    Sean___ and Pat___ home is in Dublin.
14. The sentence is a: ☐ statement   ☐ command
                        ☐ exclamation   ☐ question
    Many capital cities are interesting places.
15. Circle the pronouns.
    If we visit Dublin, you can see the famous 'Book of Kells'.
16. Circle the correct pronoun.
    Mum and I/me saw the thousand-year-old manuscript.
17. Circle the infinitive of a verb.
    St Stephen's Green and Phoenix Park, close to the city centre, are great places to relax in Dublin.
18. Write **its** or **it's**.
    Ireland is also famous for _____ traditional music and dancing.
19. Circle the noun that has common gender.
    There are many places in each county that any visitor to Ireland will enjoy.
20. Circle the expression that means do **something dangerous**.
    play with fire   strike while the iron is hot

UNIT 11

MY SCORE

MY SCORE

DAY 103

1. Circle the correct spelling.   infewsion   infusion

2. Circle the incorrect spelling.   circulate   cerculate

3. Circle the correct spelling.   resistable   resistible

4. Circle the incorrect spelling.   differculty   difficulty

5. A synonym for **rubbish** is:
   ☐ untidy   ☐ litter   ☐ landfill

6. Rearrange the letters to spell the opposite of **expand**.
   tocranct _____

7. Write the plural.
   person _____   mouse _____

8. Circle the correct homophone.
   Next weak/week is the start of the holidays.

9. Count the syllables.   because ☐   whenever ☐

10. Write the past and present participles of the verb **drop**.
    past _____   present _____

11. Who is speaking? _____
    The principal enquired, 'Where is Mr Jones?'

12. Add commas.
    Mr Jones raised his hand smiled and asked 'How can I help?'

13. Punctuate.
    mr jones was able to help the principal because he had the book she was looking for

14. Circle the proper noun.
    Cornwall is a popular holiday destination for many people.

15. Circle the word that means **rough and uneven**.
    The coastline of north Cornwall is very rugged.

16. Circle the expression that means to be suspicious.
    to smell a rat   to face the music

17. Circle the verbs. How many? ☐
    In the past, ships foundered on Cornwall's north coast and attackers stole any valuables.

18. Circle and write the collective noun. _____
    The army sought information.

19. The underlined word is a: ☐ pronoun   ☐ adverb
    Smugglers were a greater problem for the army because they were much more secretive.

20. Circle the infinitive of a verb
    The army tried everything to capture the smugglers.

DAY 104

1. Circle the incorrect spelling.   harth   hearth

2. Circle the correct spelling.   greive   grieve

3. Circle the incorrect spelling.   century   centery

4. Circle the correct spelling.   decermal   decimal

5. An antonym for **valuable** is:
   ☐ invaluable   ☐ poor   ☐ worthless

6. Change each noun to an adjective ending in **ive**.
   explosion   _____
   investigation   _____

7. **check** or **cheque**? _____
   Did you .... that the back door is locked?

8. Write an synonym for **sly**.   c_____

9. Listed alphabetically, the last word is _____.
   yoghurt   yolk   yoga   yoke

10. Circle the word that does not belong in the word family.
    vocal   vocalise   voice   vogue

11. Add the apostrophe.
    Peter and Janes holidays had begun.

12. Add apostrophes.
    Peters and Janes bags were packed.

13. Add the **apostrophe(s)** and the **letter s** if needed.
    Peter__ and Jane__ holiday will be busy.

14. The sentence is a: ☐ statement   ☐ command
    ☐ exclamation   ☐ question
    Why are the Pennine hills called the backbone of England?

15. Circle the expression that means **to ignore**.
    to keep up appearances   to give the cold shoulder

16. Circle the correct word.
    Please give them/those maps to me.

17. Circle the superlative adjective.
    The Pennine Way, one of Britain's most popular walking routes, is 429 km long.

18. Circle the conjunction.
    We always stay at youth hostels whenever we walk the Pennine Way.

19. Circle the definite article.
    The scenery of the Pennine Way is so beautiful, everyone should try to walk it.

20. Circle the infinitives.
    To tackle the whole walk in one go, you would have to be very fit.

UNIT 11

MY SCORE

MY SCORE

DAY 105

1. Circle the correct spelling.   written   writtern

2. Circle the incorrect spelling.   beggar   begger

3. Circle the correct spelling.   anniversary   anniversery

4. Circle the incorrect spelling.   cereal   cereul

5. A synonym for **secure** is:
   ☐ tight   ☐ safe   ☐ sound

6. Circle the word in which **fra(ct)** does not mean **break**.
   fraction   fracture   fragrant   fragment

7. Write the plural.
   woman _____   louse _____

8. Circle the correct homophone.
   Farmers sew/sow seeds in the springtime.

9. Count the syllables.
   nevertheless ☐   alternatively ☐

10. Write the past and present participles of the verb **drag**.
    past _____   present _____

11. Add speech marks.
    How far away is the sun? asked Dan. I want to know.

12. Add commas.
    Looking at him Mum replied 'Very very very far away!'

13. Punctuate.
    dan wanted to be an astronaut more than anything else.

14. Write **longer** or **longest**.
    Of the Amazon, the Nile and the Yangtze, which
    river is the _____?

15. Circle and write the comparative adjective. _____
    At almost 6500 km, the Amazon is very long, but the Nile is more than 250 km longer.

16. Circle the word that gives a comparison between the two rivers.
    The Nile flows through five countries, but/otherwise the Amazon flows through six.

17. Circle the verb group.
    It has been determined by scientists that the Amazon River's source is in the mountains of Peru.

18. Write **its** or **it's**.
    People of the Amazon understand _____ wildlife.

19. Circle the error.
    Do you know anything about the amazon?

20. Circle the expression.
    Destruction of the rainforests needs to be knocked on the head.

DAY 106

1. Circle the incorrect spelling.   disobey   disobay

2. Circle the correct spelling.   optician   opticern

3. Circle the incorrect spelling.   poisonous   poisernous

4. Circle the correct spelling.   trickt   tricked

5. An antonym for **poverty** is: ☐ happiness ☐ wealth

6. **tide** or **tied**? _____ .
   The string was .... around the branch.

7. **coarse** or **course**? _____
   The .... material of their skirts made their legs itch.

8. Which word means **a part of something**?
   peace   piece

9. Listed alphabetically, the second word is _____ .
   tranquil   trailer   trample   traitor

10. Circle the word that does not belong in the word family.
    revive   vitality   vivacious   vixen

11. Add the apostrophe.
    Rick and Lauras parents were worried about them.

12. Add apostrophes.
    Ricks and Lauras lives were about to change.

13. Add the **apostrophe(s)** and the **letter s** if needed.
    Rick___ and Laura___ new home was far away.

14. The sentence is a: ☐ statement   ☐ command
    ☐ exclamation   ☐ question
    Research for information on railways.

15. Circle the adverb.
    Although the Industrial Revolution began in England, it spread quickly to Western Europe.

16. Circle the verbs.
    The railways, introduced in the 1820s, were a key factor in the spread of the Industrial Revolution.

17. Circle the conjunction that occurs in pairs.
    The railways not only changed the working lives of the population but also their social lives.

18. The underlined word is: ☐ a pronoun.
    ☐ a conjunction.
    Manual labour gave way to machines so many people lost their jobs.

19. Circle the plural nouns.
    The population of many towns exploded as people came looking for work in big factories.

20. Circle the abstract noun.
    There were many diseases in towns.

MY SCORE

MY SCORE

DAY 107

1. Circle the correct spelling.   disapprove   diserprove
2. Circle the incorrect spelling.   examine   examin
3. Circle the correct spelling.   overtaken   ovataken
4. Circle the incorrect spelling.   mercyful   merciful
5. A synonym for **purchase** is: ◯ buy   ◯ sell
6. Rearrange the letters to spell the opposite of **captivity**.
   mefedor _____
7. Write the plural.
   tooth _____   child _____
8. Circle the correct homophone.
   A leak/leek is a type of vegetable.
9. Count the syllables.   however ▢   therefore ▢
10. Write the past and present participles of the verb **stop**.
    past _____   present _____
11. Add speech marks.
    After reading the story of Romulus and Remus, the teacher asked, Do you think it's fact or fiction?
12. Add commas.
    A child shot up waved his hand in the air and cried 'Sir Sir I know the answer!'
13. Punctuate.
    the children were learning about the pharaohs gods and rituals of ancient egypt
14. Circle and write the proper noun. _____
    Rome is loved by every person who visits it.
15. Circle and write the proper adjective. _____
    Legend says that Rome was built by Romulus and Remus, sons of the Roman god of war.
16. Circle the phrase that shows there could be some truth in the legend.
    Although we doubt the twins were raised by a wolf, a town did exist on the site before the Roman Empire began.
17. Write another word for huge. _____
    Two thousand years ago, the Roman Empire covered a vast area.
18. Circle the expression that means **not well**.
    out of sorts   beside oneself
19. Circle the adverb.
    Much evidence of the Roman Empire still exists.
20. Circle the preposition.
    The Romans built many great cities in their empire.

MY SCORE

DAY 108

1. Circle the incorrect spelling.   oparate   operate
2. Circle the correct spelling.   electrical   electrercal
3. Circle the incorrect spelling.   teleperthy   telepathy
4. Circle the correct spelling.   session   seshern
5. An antonym for **concrete** is:
   ◯ cement   ◯ abstract   ◯ steel
6. Change each noun to an adjective ending in **ive**.
   extension _____
   imagination _____
7. **tide** or **tied**? _____
   The .... is moving up the beach.
8. Which word means **a blood vessel**?
   vain   vein   vane
9. Listed alphabetically, the first word is _____.
   spanner   sparse   sparkle   spatula
10. Circle the word that does not belong in the word family.
    evacuate   vacant   vacation   vaccine
11. Add the apostrophe.
    George and Henrys servants spoilt the boys.
12. Add apostrophes.
    Georges and Henrys meals were cooked by the royal chef.
13. Add the **apostrophe(s)** and the **letter s** if needed.
    George__ and Henry__ parents were the king and queen.
14. The sentence is a: ◯ statement   ◯ command
                         ◯ exclamation   ◯ question
    That is the most ridiculous excuse I've heard!
15. Circle and write the pronouns. _____
    You ought to be ashamed of yourself!
16. Circle the expression.
    In my day, many moons ago, your punishment would have been severe!
17. Circle the conjunction that occurs in a pair.
    Not only are you telling untruths but also you are laughing about it!
18. Write the two verbs. _____
    The boy picked up his catapult and aimed it at the window.
19. Circle the noun that has common gender.
    One child in the class gasped in disbelief at his cheek.
20. Circle the expression.
    That behaviour was nipped in the bud by the teacher.

MY SCORE

DAY 109

1. Circle the correct spelling. genrerly generally

2. Circle the incorrect spelling. impress imppress

3. Circle the correct spelling. dreamer dremer

4. Circle the incorrect spelling. painkiller painkilla

5. A synonym for *mistake* is:
   ◯ error   ◯ identify   ◯ crime

6. Circle the word in which *herb* does not mean *plant*.

   herbal   herbicide   herbivorous   hereby

7. Write the plural.

   formula _____   foot _____

8. Circle the correct homophone.
   The new root/route to Dublin reduces traffic jams.

9. Count the syllables.

   meanwhile ◻   consequently ◻

10. Write the past and present participles of the verb *hug*.

    past _____   present _____

11. Add speech marks.

    Will we be able to sail this afternoon? Alan asked. It
    looks a bit rough to me.

12. Add commas.

    Alan enjoyed many sports: tennis indoor cricket
    badminton basketball and swimming.

13. Punctuate.

    Alan bought a book about sports called sports fanatic

14. Write the correct word. this that

    I have swum at _____ beach but I prefer this
    one.

15. Circle the word that intensifies *windy*.

    It is often too windy in the afternoon.

16. Circle the phrase in the second sentence that connects
    the two sentences.

    Marco wanted to improve his surfing skills. For that
    reason, he went to the beach every morning.

17. Circle the verb group.

    Marco, along with his two best friends, has been in the
    surf club since he was very young.

18. Circle the two prepositions.

    The high waves kept people away from the sea so they
    walked on the sand.

19. Circle the correct verb.

    But Marco, unlike his friends, was/were never put off by
    bad conditions.

20. Circle the noun with common gender.

    Marco and his friend love the local beach.

DAY 110

1. Circle the incorrect spelling. surch search

2. Circle the correct spelling. roumer rumour

3. Circle the incorrect spelling. public publick

4. Circle the correct spelling. trayner trainer

5. An antonym for *begin* is:
   ◯ initial   ◯ cease   ◯ commence

6. Change each noun to an adjective ending in *ive*.

   corrosion _____

   information _____

7. *missed* or *mist*? _____
   Have you .... the bus?

8. Which word means *an increase in money*?

   profit   prophet

9. Listed alphabetically, the third word is _____.
   siesta   sieve   sideboard   significant

10. Circle the word that does not belong in the word family.
    attract   traction   tractor   tracksuit

11. Add the apostrophe.

    Bek and Toms family enjoyed a healthy lifestyle.

12. Add apostrophes.

    Beks and Toms bicycles were well-used.

13. Add the *apostrophe(s)* and the *letter s* if needed.

    Bek___ and Tom___ brother was a top triathlete.

14. The sentence is a: ◻ statement   ◻ command
    ◻ exclamation   ◻ question
    Does cycling keep you fit and healthy?

15. Circle the verb group for the verb *to cycle*.

    If you ride a short distance each day, you will have
    cycled a long way by the end of the year.

16. Circle the proper adjective.

    Bek and Tom cycle around the lakes on their Italian
    bikes their parents bought for them.

17. Circle the conjunction.

    They cycle a long way yet, they are having so much fun,
    they don't notice the distance.

18. Circle the noun with common gender.

    Tom likes to cycle with his cousin.

19. Complete the simile in this sentence.

    Mum likes to relax and always cycles as slow as a

    _____ .

20. Circle and write the abstract noun. _____

    The whole family's fitness has improved.

1. Circle the correct spelling.   boredom   bordom

2. Circle the incorrect spelling. transver   transfer

3. Circle the correct spelling.   abbreviation   abbrieviation

4. Circle the incorrect spelling. argument   arguement

5. A synonym for **elevate** is:
   ☐ alleviate   ☐ raise   ☐ elegant

6. Use the prefixes **mal** and **mis** to make two new words.
   adjustment _____
   adventure _____

7. Write the plural or singular of each word.
   index _____   scissors _____

8. Circle the correct homophone.
   The tiger's paw/pour required the vet's attention.

9. Count the syllables. anticipate ☐ antiseptic ☐

10. Write the adverb from the adjective **pretty**.
    adverb _____

11. Add the apostrophes.
    Tims ankle was sprained when he fell off the twins trampoline.

12. Write the contraction after each underlined phrase.
    Tim <u>did not</u> _____ want to cry but he <u>could not</u> _____ help it.

13. Punctuate.
    the doctor gave tim pain killers bandages and crutches to help his injury

14. Circle the prepositions.
    For a while, Tim needed to walk with crutches.

15. The underlined word has:
    ☐ masculine gender   ☐ common gender
    Tim's <u>doctor</u> advised against playing sport for a few weeks.

16. Circle the definite article.
    Tim takes off the bandages after two weeks.

17. Add the past tense of the verb **to feel**.
    Tim's memory of the fall and the pain he _____ is still very clear.

18. Complete the simile.
    After some time and a lot of rest, he was as fit as a _____ .

19. Circle two nouns with common gender.
    Tim received sympathetic messages from his best friend and his teacher.

20. Circle and write the reflexive pronoun. _____
    When he was on crutches, Tim's mum encouraged him to do as much as possible himself.

1. Circle the incorrect spelling.   prevous   previous

2. Circle the correct spelling.   quarrel   quarell

3. Circle the incorrect spelling.   cercus   circus

4. Circle the correct spelling.   acquatic   aquatic

5. An antonym for **unite** is:
   ☐ union   ☐ divert   ☐ divide

6. Write each word with the suffix **ial** or **ular**.
   office _____   single _____

7. **tail** or **tale**? _____
   Granny always has an interesting .... to tell.

8. Which word means to interfere?
   medal   meddle

9. Listed alphabetically, the last word is _____ .
   oblivious   oblique   obliterate   objective

10. Circle the word that does not belong in the word group.
    generous   generosity   generation   generously

11. Add one comma.
    Mum called loudly 'Lunch is ready!'

12. Add the commas.
    Mum had prepared nachos spring rolls sushi and a fruit platter.

13. Circle the infinitive.
    Everyone rushed to the table and began to eat hungrily.

14. Circle and write the adverb. _____
    Some cheap modern furniture is badly made.

15. Insert **it's** or **its**.
    Many people prefer to buy old, well-made furniture and restore it to _____ former glory.

16. Circle the word that means **items of good value**.
    Excellent bargains can be found in antique shops.

17. Circle and write the conjunction. _____
    Wooden furniture needs to be sanded down to remove layers of varnish before it can be restored.

18. Insert the better word.   courage   patience
    Restoring furniture by hand takes a great deal of dedication, time and _____ .

19. Add the same ending.
    Some people say restor_____ furniture is a relax_____ and reward_____ hobby.

20. Insert a suitable word.
    People who make furniture by hand _____ it for a high price.

MY SCORE

MY SCORE

UNIT 12

1. Circle the correct spelling.   dependibility   dependability
2. Circle the incorrect spelling.   accurate   acurrate
3. Circle the correct spelling.   cowoperate   cooperate
4. Circle the incorrect spelling.   incident   incerdent
5. A synonym for **cure** is:
   ☐ manage   ☐ remedy   ☐ protect
6. Use the prefixes **mal** or **mis** to make a new word.
   function _____
7. Write the plural.
   scissors _____
8. Circle the correct homophone.
   The <u>tail/tale</u> of the ancient mariner is a long poem.
9. Count the syllables.   barrister ☐   bayonet ☐
10. Write the adverb from the adjective **happy**.
    adverb _____
11. Add the apostrophes.
    Abdul and Abels parents visited the sultans palace.
12. Write the contractions of the two underlined phrases.
    _____   _____
    <u>They had</u> never seen such beauty and now <u>they are</u> renovating their home in the same style.
13. Add **Its** or **It's**.
    Abdul and Abel are not sure they like the new
    style. _____ much too glamorous for them.
14. The underlined word is a: ☐ verb.
    ☐ noun.
    The land <u>ruled</u> by a sultan is called his sultanate and_ his queen is called the sultana.
15. Circle the masculine noun.
    Sultans of the Ottoman Empire ruled over parts of Europe, Asia and Africa for more than 600 years.
16. Circle the word that links this sentence to the previous one.
    Consequently, there is a great architectural legacy of this empire in these regions.
17. The underlined word is an _____ noun.
    The Ottoman Empire ended with the <u>defeat</u> of its allies after World War I.
18. The verb is: ☐ present tense. ☐ past tense.
    The Republic of Turkey <u>was born</u> from the ashes of the Ottoman Empire.
19. The pronoun refers to _____.
    The greater part of Turkey is in Asia, but some of <u>it</u> is in Europe.
20. Circle and write the verb. _____
    Anzac Cove, which is on the Gallipoli Peninsula, is in Turkey.

1. Circle the incorrect spelling.   sovreign   sovereign
2. Circle the correct spelling.   annual   anual
3. Circle the incorrect spelling.   celebritty   celebrity
4. Circle the correct spelling.   latitude   latertude
5. An antonym for **majority** is:
   ☐ major   ☐ minor   ☐ minority
6. Write each word with the suffix **ial** or **ular**.
   angle _____   part _____
7. **tail** or **tale**? _____
   Never stand on an animal's ....
8. Which word means a dried fruit? _____
   current   currant
9. Listed alphabetically, the second word is _____.
   palette   palace   pallet   palate
10. Circle the word that does not belong in the word group.
    agreeable   agreeably   aggressive   agreement
11. Add two commas.
    As he resurfaced the troll spluttered and screeched angrily 'You will be sorry you ever crossed me!'
12. Add two commas.
    Gryphon Gawblr and Garmen stared down as the troll climbed up the rickety wooden bridge.
13. Add commas to clarify meaning.
    Gryphon the largest goat with the biggest horns knocked the troll back into the river.
14. Circle the verbs.
    The troll made ripples that spread across the river.
15. Circle the three prepositions.
    The three goats danced across the bridge to the lush green grass on the opposite bank.
16. Circle the conjunction.
    The goats took one last look at the river before they began eating.
17. Circle the better verb.   see   hear
    As they ate, they could _____ the troll squelching up the slippery riverbank.
18. Pick **nothing** or **anything**.
    As he walked across the grass, the troll could
    think of _____ but revenge.
19. Circle the negative verb group.
    The goats were enjoying their grassy meal so much they did not hear the troll approach.
20. Circle the noun the pronouns refer to.
    The troll growled at the smallest goat, who bolted to the bridge, taking the others with him.

MY SCORE

MY SCORE

UNIT 12

1. Circle the correct spelling.   pertition   petition
2. Circle the incorrect spelling.   labratory   laboratory
3. Circle the correct spelling.   telergraph   telegraph
4. Circle the incorrect spelling.   boundry   boundary
5. A synonym for **bravery** is:
   ☐ courage   ☐ strength   ☐ willpower
6. Use the prefixes **mal** and **mis** to make two new words.
   fortune _____   nutrition _____
7. Write the plural or singular of each word.
   bacteria _____   gateau _____
8. Circle the correct homophone.
   The hour/our has come for hour/our birthday party.
9. Count the syllables.   caviar ☐   civilised ☐
10. Write the adverb from the adjective **heavy**.
    adverb _____
11. Add the apostrophes.
    Coras and Rachels birthdays are in the same month as their parents wedding anniversary.
12. Write the contraction next to the underlined phrase.
    The sisters could have _____ had joint celebrations, but they did not _____ want to.
13. Punctuate.
    Rachel is collecting the cake confirmed Cora.
14. Insert the correct form of the verb **to be**.
    In medieval times, people accused of particular crimes _____ subject to 'trial by ordeal'.
15. Insert a suitable word.
    The accused suffered great physical _____ during these trials.
16. The verb is: ☐ present tense. ☐ past tense.
    It was believed that if innocent, they would be protected from harm.
17. The word **ordeal** means:
    ☐ a severe and testing experience.
    ☐ numbers placed in order.
18. Circle the better word.   unsafe   unjust
    This was such an _____ system to follow.
19. The underlined verb is in the _____ tense.
    Those who were guilty confessed, but sadly the innocent suffered.
20. Circle and write the reflexive pronoun. _____
    During witch-hunts an innocent woman would not be able to save herself.

1. Circle the incorrect spelling.   armour   armer
2. Circle the correct spelling.   thiefs   thieves
3. Circle the incorrect spelling.   feiry   fiery
4. Circle the correct spelling.   education   edgercation
5. An antonym for **expand** is:
   ☐ increase   ☐ contract   ☐ miniscule
6. Write each word with the suffix **ial** or **ular**.
   finance _____   spectacle _____
7. **imaginary** or **imaginative**? _____
   Sophie writes very .... stories.
8. The word **attempt** comes from the Latin word **temptare** meaning   ☐ to finish   ☐ to try
9. Listed alphabetically, the first word is _____.
   realise   reassure   reaction   reasonable
10. Circle the word that does not belong in the word group.
    decide   decipher   decision   decisive
11. Add two commas.
    Moving forward in a trance Barry spoke in a voice so unlike his own 'Who will walk with me to the centre of the maze?'
12. Add a comma or commas.
    Don stepped forward knowing only he could save this poor boy from the evil witch Bellamort.
13. Add commas to clarify meaning.
    Don took Barry's wand and crossed it with his own an inferior model as they entered the maze.
14. Circle and write the proper noun. _____
    The first Tour de France was contested in 1903.
15. Circle the infinitive.
    In the early years, the riders rode through the night to complete the stages.
16. Circle the word meaning competitors.
    Because the race was so difficult, some riders cheated to get an advantage over their rivals.
17. Circle the word that means **steps in a process**.
    The first race was almost 3000 km long, but it had six stages: six very long stages!
18. The underlined word is a: ☐ conjunction.
    ☐ preposition.
    The race was the idea of a magazine journalist and his editor.
19. Circle and write the verb. _____
    This popular tour experienced many drug scandals.
20. Circle the superlative adjective.
    The Tour de France is one of the most important stage races in the cycling calendar.

UNIT 12

DAY 117

1. Circle the correct spelling. discerpline discipline

2. Circle the incorrect spelling. responsable responsible

3. Circle the correct spelling. suspect suspeckt

4. Circle the incorrect spelling. hemersphere hemisphere

5. A synonym for *exhibit* is:
   ☐ exhale   ☐ display   ☐ displace

6. Use the prefixes *mal* and *mis* to make two new words.

   giving _____   practice _____

7. Write the plural or singular of each word.

   goose _____   oxen _____

8. Circle the correct homophone.
   The mung bean/been can be used in sweet and savoury dishes.

9. Count the syllables. decipher ☐ distribute ☐

10. Write the adverb from the adjective *lazy*.

    adverb _____

11. Add the apostrophes.
    The childrens toys were found by the babys cot.

12. Write the contraction next to the underlined phrase.

    Someone must have _____ seen who

    had _____ put them there.

13. Punctuate.
    Stop Thief shouted the shop manager

14. Circle the common noun.
    The suburb of Wimbledon is in South-West London.

15. Circle the proper nouns.
    The suburb is famous for two things: Wombles, who live beneath Wimbledon Common, and tennis.

16. Insert a suitable word.
    The tennis makes the news for two weeks but the

    Wombles collect rubbish all _____ round.

17. Write *public* or *private*.
    Wimbledon Common is a _____ park, preserved for wildlife and is available for everyone to enjoy.

18. Circle the word meaning *respected* and *important*.
    The Wimbledon tennis club has existed since 1877 and its annual tournament is the most prestigious in the tennis calendar.

19. Circle the two verb groups.
    Tennis began in France but the hand was used to hit the ball; racquets were used first in England.

20. *on* or *in*? _____
    The author of the Wombles novels, Elizabeth Beresford, based the characters .... members of her family.

DAY 118

1. Circle the incorrect spelling. attenttion attention

2. Circle the correct spelling. magnet magnut

3. Circle the incorrect spelling. childish childesh

4. Circle the correct spelling. superiur superior

5. An antonym for *profit* is:
   ☐ prophet   ☐ lose   ☐ loss

6. Write each word with the suffix *ial* or *ular*.

   circle _____   confidence _____

7. *instance* or *instanf*? _____
   In this ...., I will accept your excuse, but next time, beware!

8. Which word means *a part of the body*?
   waist   waste

9. Listed alphabetically, the third word is _____.
   scamper   scalpel   scarcely   scavenger

10. Circle the word that does not belong in the word group.
    imagination   imitate   imaginative   imagine

11. Add three commas.
    Tina wondered aloud 'What shall I buy my best beautiful funny friend for her birthday?'

12. Add three commas.
    Tina had plenty of ideas as her friend loved drawing craft calligraphy reading and stationery.

13. The underlined word is a:
    ☐ proper noun   ☐ proper adjective
    We are going to learn about French history.

14. Circle and write the verb group. _____
    The guillotine was named after Joseph Guillotin, the French doctor who invented it.

15. Circle the better word. feature method
    It was designed as a quick, less traumatic

    _____ of execution.

16. Circle the better word. reason purpose
    The _____ of capital punishment was to end life, not inflict pain.

17. The underlined word is: ☐ an adjective ☐ a verb
    At the time of the guillotine's invention, the French people were revolting against the monarchy.

18. Circle the conjunction.
    During the French Revolution, many people of the ruling classes were executed.

19. Circle and write the proper adjective. _____
    Two victims of the guillotine were King Louis XVI of France and his Austrian queen, Marie Antoinette.

20. Circle the word closest in meaning to *rebellion*.
    The Place de la Concorde is where the executions took place during the revolution.

MY SCORE

MY SCORE

UNIT 12

DAY 119

1. Circle the correct spelling.   ciclone   cyclone

2. Circle the incorrect spelling.   relertive   relative

3. Circle the correct spelling.   abandonned   abandoned

4. Circle the incorrect spelling.   convinient   convenient

5. A synonym for *ruin* is:
   ☐ wreak   ☐ wreck

6. Use the prefixes *mal* and *mis* to make two new words.
   treat _____   trust _____

7. Write the plural or singular of each word.
   cacti _____   trout _____

8. Circle the correct homophone.
   The weather vane/vein on the roof was damaged.

9. Count the syllables.   estimate ☐   evaporate ☐

10. Write the adverb from the adjective *ready*.
    adverb _____

11. Add the apostrophe.
    The hunters guns were poised, ready to fire.

12. Write the contraction next to the underlined phrase.
    They had _____ *been following a wolf,*
    unaware that they would _____ *be the targets.*

13. Punctuate.
    I think we should get out of here suggested one hunter

14. Circle the superlative adjective.
    In June and August each year, Britain's smallest town
    plays host to two unusual sporting events.

15. Circle the proper adjective.
    In June, the small Welsh town hosts the Man versus
    Horse cross-country marathon.

16. The sentence is written in the _____ tense.
    Horse and rider compete against mountain bikers and
    runners; surprisingly, horses don't always win.

17. Write *is* or *are*.
    The World Bog Snorkelling Championships _____
    held in a peat bog on the outskirts of the town.

18. Circle the word meaning *muddy and dirty*.
    Competitors swim doggie-paddle through the murky
    water as they complete two laps of the trench.

19. The verb is: ☐ past tense   ☐ present tense
    The Man versus Horse race was established before the
    bog snorkelling event.

20. Circle the phrase linking this sentence to the one above.
    In addition to these unusual events, a cheese rolling
    competition is another annual event.

MY SCORE

DAY 120

1. Circle the incorrect spelling.   confewsion   confusion

2. Circle the correct spelling.   magishan   magician

3. Circle the incorrect spelling.   definately   definitely

4. Circle the correct spelling.   chauffeur   chaufeur

5. An antonym for *probable* is:
   ☐ possible   ☐ definitely   ☐ doubtful

6. Write each word with the suffix *ial* or *ular*.
   muscle _____   palace _____

7. *instance* or *instant*? _____
   These are .... coffee granules.

8. The word *portal* comes from the Latin word
   porta meaning   ☐ door   ☐ left side

9. Listed alphabetically, the third word is _____.
   routine   rough   roulette   rouge

10. Circle the word that does not belong in the word group.
    fortunate   fortunately   fortitude   fortune

11. Add one comma.
    Linda muttered 'I cannot believe I'm doing this!'

12. Add two commas.
    The race had four parts: a swim an assault course a
    mountain bike ride and a cross-country run.

13. Punctuate.
    Linda exclaimed I'm delighted to be finished!

14. Circle the verb.
    During World War I, the British king changed the name
    of the British Royal Family from Saxe-Coburg-Gotha to
    Windsor.

15. Circle the proper nouns.
    Because Britain was at war with Germany, it would be
    better if the name was not German.

16. Circle the proper adjective.
    The German name had come from Prince Albert,
    the husband of Queen Victoria, who was the king's
    grandfather.

17. Circle the word meaning *ruler*.
    Albert and Victoria's daughter married the German
    emperor; they had a son named Wilhelm.

18. Present or past tense? _____
    When his father died, Wilhelm became ruler of the
    German Empire.

19. *they're* or *their*?
    Although Britain and Germany were on opposite sides
    during WWI, _____ *kings were first cousins.*

20. Circle the abstract noun.
    Because of the bitterness felt towards Germany, King
    George changed his family's name.

MY SCORE

UNIT 12

1. Circle the correct spelling.   allience   alliance
2. Circle the incorrect spelling.   vertical   verticul
3. Circle the correct spelling.   embarassed   embarrassed
4. Circle the incorrect spelling.   similer   similar
5. A synonym for **increase** is:
   ☐ decrease   ☐ export   ☐ expand
6. Use the prefixes **inter** and **trans** to make two new words.
   action _____   section _____
7. Write the plural or singular of each word.
   leaves _____   fish _____
8. Circle the correct homophones.
   I know what to <u>wear/where</u> and <u>wear/where</u> to go.
9. Count the syllables.   fascinate ☐   fuselage ☐
10. Write the adverb from the adjective **beautiful**.
    adverb _____
11. Add capital letters where needed.
    to celebrate mum's birthday, the family went for dinner at their local italian restaurant.
12. The dash shows: ☐ repetition   ☐ interruption
    'I think I'll order —'
    'Pizza and chips!' cut in Joe, in a tone of mock surprise.
13. Punctuate.
    There were four starters five mains and four desserts to choose from
14. Circle the prepositions.
    In the Middle Ages, trade between China and Western Europe, and all the places in between, occurred along the Silk Route.
15. Circle the word closest in meaning to **infection**.
    The Black Death plague travelled along the route.
16. Circle the proper noun.
    The plague killed millions of people in Europe.
17. The underlined word is: ☐ an adverb.
    ☐ a preposition.
    The plague was passed <u>on</u> to humans bitten by infected fleas.
18. **was** or **were**?
    Other types of plague _____ passed on through infected blood, and coughing and sneezing.
19. The underlined words are: ☐ adverbs.
    ☐ prepositions.
    The bodies of victims were collected <u>at</u> night <u>by</u> men wheeling carts <u>through</u> the streets.
20. The sentence is in the _____ tense.
    Their bodies were piled into mass graves.

MY SCORE

1. Circle the incorrect spelling.   carridge   carriage
2. Circle the correct spelling.   obediant   obedient
3. Circle the incorrect spelling.   suspicion   suspiscion
4. Circle the correct spelling.   athsma   asthma
5. An antonym for **tranquil** is:
   ☐ calm   ☐ peaceful   ☐ stormy
6. Add the suffix **ment** to give the noun.
   enjoy _____   judge _____
7. **its** or **it's**? _____
   The eagle couldn't soar with .... injured wing.
8. Which word means **to look without blinking**? _____
   stair   stare
9. Listed alphabetically, the third word is _____ .
   antler   anxious   anxiety   antique
10. Circle the word that does not belong in the word group.
    applicable   applicant   applaud   application
11. Which adjective phrase needs a hyphen?
    ☐ *The actor was <u>well known</u>.*
    ☐ *He was a <u>well known</u> actor.*
12. Add a hyphen.
    I drank one third of my juice.
13. Add a hyphen.
    The play has been running for sixty five years.
14. Circle the word that means **got rid of**.
    Slavery in the United States was abolished at the end of the civil war (1861–1865).
15. The pronoun refers to which noun? _____
    The opposing sides were the southern states, who were for slavery, and the northern states, who were against <u>it</u>.
16. Insert **to** or **from**.
    The southern states had separated _____ the union of states before the war began.
17. Circle the plural nouns.
    The southern states which used slaves in their cotton fields thought nations that bought their cotton would support them.
18. Circle and write the definite article. _____
    The southern states received help from no-one.
19. Circle the conjunction that connects the sentences.
    Eleven of the 15 slave states separated from the United States, but 13 were represented on the Confederate States flag.
20. Circle the word that is not needed.
    Abraham Lincoln was the president of the United States during the civil war began.

MY SCORE

DAY 123

1. Circle the correct spelling. pecussion **percussion**

2. Circle the incorrect spelling. separately **seprately**

3. Circle the correct spelling. desolve **dissolve**

4. Circle the incorrect spelling. interval **intervul**

5. A synonym for **visitor** is:

   ☐ visual ☐ guessed ☐ guest

6. Use the prefixes **inter** and **trans** to make two new words.

   change _____ script _____

7. Write the plural or singular of each word.

   bottle _____ series _____

8. Circle the correct homophones.

   There won't be any peace/piece until the last peace/
   piece of cake has been eaten!

9. Count the syllables. geography ☐ glossary ☐

10. Write the adverb from the adjective **curious**.

    adverb _____

11. Add capital letters where needed.

    the stanton circus gave its last show on friday.

12. The dash shows: ☐ repetition ☐ interruption
    'The circus is just so—so amazing!' cried David.

13. Add commas if needed.

    The two-hour show had trapeze artists jugglers acrobats
    and clowns.

14. Circle the two superlative adjectives.

    Mount Kilimanjaro is the highest mountain on the
    African continent and the tallest freestanding mountain
    in the world.

15. Circle the noun the pronoun **each** refers to.

    Climbing Kilimanjaro takes you through five ecological
    zones, each about 1000 m in altitude.

16. **Changes** is a: ☐ noun ☐ verb.

    The climate changes from tropical at the mountain's base
    to arctic at its summit, Uhuru Point.

17. Circle the verb.

    The snow-capped Mount Kilimanjaro, which is in
    Tanzania, east Africa, is very close to the equator.

18. The underlined word is an:

    ☐ adjective ☐ abstract noun

    Kilimanjaro is a volcanic mountain with three volcanic
    cones: Kibo, Mawenzi and Shira.

19. Circle the conjunction.

    Mawenzi and Shira are extinct but Kibo is dormant.

20. Circle the pronoun that refers to the noun.

    Kilimanjaro has a huge area of glacial ice at its peak,
    but this is receding.

DAY 124

1. Circle the incorrect spelling. association **asociation**

2. Circle the correct spelling. **oxygen** oxergen

3. Circle the incorrect spelling. conscientious **consientous**

4. Circle the correct spelling. litrature **literature**

5. An antonym for **derelict** is:

   ☐ devastated ☐ cared-for ☐ careless

6. Add the suffix **ment** to give the noun.

   adjust _____ encourage _____

7. **right** or **rite**? _____

   Is this the .... direction to the cinema?

8. Write an antonym for **superior**. i_____

9. Listed alphabetically, the first word is _____ .

   bandage banish bandit banjo

10. Circle the word that does not belong in the word group.

    effective effectively effigy effectiveness

11. Which adjective phrase needs a hyphen?

    ☐ *The young boy has fair hair.*
    ☐ *He was a fair haired young boy.*

12. Add a hyphen.

    Mimi ate three quarters of the large pizza.

13. Add a hyphen.

    They celebrated twenty five years of marriage.

14. Circle the three proper nouns.

    Sri Lanka is an island nation lying in the Indian Ocean
    just east of the southern tip of India.

15. Circle the word which means attackers.

    Since people first arrived on the island, Sri Lanka has
    seen many invaders and political changes.

16. Circle the verb group.

    Buddhism came to Sri Lanka in the third century BC and
    a great city was established in the north.

17. Circle the word that means a large area of the world.

    After one thousand years, another city took control
    of the region and the great shrine to Buddhism was
    abandoned.

18. Circle the pronoun that relates to **the island**.

    Ancient Greeks and Romans traded with the people of
    the island and Arab traders settled there from the eighth
    century.

19. Circle the proper adjectives.

    Later, the Portuguese then the Dutch and then the
    British came to the shores of Sri Lanka.

20. Circle the verb group.

    In 1972, the country became a republic and changed
    its name to Sri Lanka; before then, it had been known
    as Ceylon.

UNIT 13

1. Circle the correct spelling.　emotion　emocean
2. Circle the incorrect spelling.　parralell　parallel
3. Circle the correct spelling.　distribution　distrabution
4. Circle the incorrect spelling.　senery　scenery
5. A synonym for *exit* is:
   ☐ extreme　☐ department　☐ departure
6. Use the prefixes *inter* and *trans* to make two new words.
   action _____　formation _____
7. Write the plural or singular of each word.
   deer _____　thieves _____
8. Circle the correct homophones.
   To higher/hire the costume he wanted, Anton had to pay a higher/hire price.
9. Count the syllables.　herbivore ☐　hesitate ☐
10. Write the adverb and noun from the adjective *disastrous*.
    adverb _____　noun _____
11. Add capital letters where needed.
    earth is known as the blue planet.
12. Punctuate.
    can you name the five oceans asked the teacher
13. Punctuate.
    I can I can bragged Aoife.
14. Circle the two verbs.
    The Blue Dragon Children's Foundation is a charity that helps disadvantaged children in Vietnam.
15. Can you spot a mistake? ☐ yes　☐ no
    These children may have disabilities or be victims of poverty human trafficking and slavery.
16. Circle a word that means *work*.
    Breaking the poverty cycle, through education and employment opportunities, is the foundation's main aim.
17. Circle and write the abstract noun. _____
    Many children have been given hope.
18. Circle the two plural nouns.
    Many street kids live and work on the streets with no protection from the weather or the ever-present danger of violence.
19. Circle the verb group.
    The Foundation was established in 2002.
20. Circle the preposition.
    Michael offers regular lessons and support to many children.

1. Circle the incorrect spelling.　discription　description
2. Circle the correct spelling.　medjieval　medieval
3. Circle the incorrect spelling.　apperatus　apparatus
4. Circle the correct spelling.　reference　refrence
5. An antonym for *lament* is:
   ☐ lame　☐ moan　☐ rejoice
6. Add the suffix *ment* to give the noun.
   attach _____　engage _____
7. *famous* or *noticeable*? _____
   The visitor to the school was a .... politician.
8. Write a synonym for *buy*.　p_____
9. Listed alphabetically, the second word is _____.
   falter　falcon　fallow　false
10. Circle the word that does not belong in the word group.
    appear　appeal　appearance　appearing
11. Which adjective phrase needs a hyphen?
    ☐ *She was a bad tempered teacher.*
    ☐ *The teacher was bad tempered.*
12. Add a hyphen.
    About one half of the class voted in favour.
13. Add a hyphen.
    My brother had a party for his twenty first birthday.
14. Circle and write the verb group. _____
    Born in 1982, Nick Vujicic has lived his life without limbs.
15. Circle the correct word.　excepted　accepted
    Although his early life was a great struggle, Nick eventually .... his condition and looked at the positives in his life.
16. Circle the infinitive.
    Nick has worked hard to live a full life, conquering the life skills that most people do without even thinking.
17. Circle the conjunction.
    Nick was born in Melbourne, Australia but now lives in California in the United States.
18. Circle the conjunction.
    Since graduating from university, Nick has had a full-time career as a motivational speaker.
19. Circle the word meaning *great interest and passion*.
    Nick has visited more than 25 countries, sharing his experiences and enthusiasm for life.
20. Circle the proper noun.
    The medical name for the condition which Nick has is tetra-amelia syndrome.

UNIT 13

MY SCORE

MY SCORE

1. Circle the correct spelling.   variety   varietty
2. Circle the incorrect spelling.   cemerony   ceremony
3. Circle the correct spelling.   burgler   burglar
4. Circle the incorrect spelling.   sensible   sensable
5. A synonym for **abundant** is:
   ☐ absurd   ☐ ample   ☐ amplify
6. Use the prefixes **inter** and **trans** to make two new words.
   mission _____   national _____
7. Write the plural or singular of each word.
   formulae _____   yolk _____
8. Circle the correct homophones.
   We're/weir going to look at the _we're/weir_.
9. Count the syllables. instrument ☐ isosceles ☐
10. Write the adverb and noun from the adjective **dangerous**.
    adverb _____   noun _____
11. Add capital letters where needed.
    the largest planet in our solar system is jupiter.
12. Punctuate.
    We are going to learn about the solar system announced the teacher.
13. Punctuate.
    The children asked when are we going to start
14. Circle the mistake.
    The Vikings were invading warriors who came from Denmark Norway and Sweden.
15. Circle the word that means a long period of years.
    The Viking era lasted for about 400 years.
16. The underlined words is: ☐ an infinitive. ☐ a pronoun.
    Some Vikings visited other lands to steal what they could; others wanted to settle there.
17. How many proper nouns? ☐
    The Vikings sailed west to North America, east to Russia and south to the Mediterranean.
18. Circle the verb group.
    Vikings settled in parts of Britain; the Irish capital, Dublin was founded by the Vikings.
19. Circle the noun the pronoun refers to.
    The Vikings attacked monasteries in Britain because they had great wealth and no defences.
20. Circle the adjectives that describe the longships.
    The Vikings' longships were narrow, light wooden vessels built for speed.

MY SCORE

1. Circle the incorrect spelling.   audable   audible
2. Circle the correct spelling.   rhoobarb   rhubarb
3. Circle the incorrect spelling.   progect   project
4. Circle the correct spelling.   formula   formular
5. An antonym for **liberty** is:
   ☐ mirage   ☐ gloom   ☐ captivity
6. Add the suffix **ment** to give the noun.
   amuse _____   develop _____
7. **loose** or **lose**? _____
   His slippers were so ...., they came off his feet.
8. Which word means **a religious ceremony**?
   right   write   rite
9. Listed alphabetically, the last word is _____ .
   incense   incredible   incident   include
10. Circle the word that does not belong in the word group.
    destiny   destroy   destruction   destructive
11. Which adjective phrase needs a hyphen?
    ☐ The holiday was _much needed_.
    ☐ The _much needed_ holiday was enjoyed by all.
12. Add a hyphen.
    By Thursday afternoon, four fifths of the school week is over.
13. Add a hyphen.
    In my school, PE lessons last for thirty five minutes.
14. Circle and write the verb group. _____
    Snowflakes are composed of tiny ice crystals.
15. Which word means one-of-a-kind? _____
    Each crystal is symmetrical with a hexagonal structure, yet each one is unique.
16. Circle the noun the pronoun refers to.
    Snow is water that freezes and then crystallises in the atmosphere, where it may stay in clouds or fall as snow.
17. Circle the adverb.
    In some countries, it snows occasionally and this may be enough to cover the ground.
18. Circle the word that is not needed.
    In the other countries, it snows heavily every winter and the people are prepared for it after.
19. Circle the word meaning **a complete stop**.
    A country that experiences snow infrequently can be brought to a standstill when it is surprised by a heavy snowfall.
20. Circle the infinitive.
    Although it can affect transport, without snow, people would not be able to enjoy snow sports.

MY SCORE

UNIT 13

1. Circle the correct spelling.   conciet   conceit
2. Circle the incorrect spelling.   rehearsal   reherseal
3. Circle the correct spelling.   exsaminer   examiner
4. Circle the incorrect spelling.   nation   naition
5. A synonym for **adequate** is:
   ☐ adept   ☐ sufficient   ☐ suffocate
6. Use the prefixes **inter** and **trans** to make two new words.
   fusion _____   lock _____
7. Write the plural or singular of each word.
   church _____   buzz _____
8. Circle the correct homophones.
   Check/Cheque that the _check/cheque_ is in there.
9. Count the syllables.   jubilant ☐   justify ☐
10. Write the adverb and noun from the adjective **foolish**.
    adverb _____   noun _____
11. Add capital letters where needed.
    the rocky mountains and the andes form a chain of mountains on the west coast of the americas.
12. Use commas where needed.
    The Himalayas located in Asia separate the Tibetan plateau from the Indian subcontinent.
13. Punctuate.
    I know some information about the Himalayas added Tony
14. Circle the error.
    Arthur and his knights of the round table is a legend that some people beleive to be true.
15. Circle a word that means **sorcerer**.
    Arthur was born at Tintagel castle but, for his safety, he was sent to live with the magician, Merlin.
16. Circle and write the infinitive. _____
    Merlin sent Arthur to live with a family who had a son called Kay.
17. Circle the word that means **fixed firmly**.
    Arthur lost Kay's sword but released one that was embedded in a huge rock, and gave it to Kay.
18. Circle the pronoun.
    In pulling the sword from the stone, Arthur had proved himself to be the high king of Britain.
19. Circle the three verbs.
    Merlin took Arthur to see a friend, the lady of the lake, who gave him a special sword, Excalibur.
20. The underlined word is a: ☐ verb.
    ☐ adjective.
    Excalibur was kept in a magic scabbard that <u>protected</u> Arthur.

1. Circle the incorrect spelling.   miserable   misrable
2. Circle the correct spelling.   radeator   radiator
3. Circle the incorrect spelling.   contrabution   contribution
4. Circle the correct spelling.   prosprous   prosperous
5. An antonym for **flawed** is:
   ☐ floor   ☐ perfect   ☐ perfume
6. Add the suffix **ment** to give the noun.
   advertise _____
   disappoint _____
7. **their** or **there**? _____
   Do you know if .... daughter can swim?
8. The word **corpse** comes from the Latin word **corpus** meaning   ☐ body   ☐ reading
9. Listed alphabetically, the second word is _____.
   liberty   liability   lichen   licence
10. Circle the word that does not belong in the word group.
    curious   curiosity   curtain   curiously
11. Which adjective phrase needs a hyphen?
    ☐ _Children enjoy many activities <u>after</u> <u>school</u>._
    ☐ _Children enjoy many <u>after school</u> activities._
12. Add a hyphen.
    We are awake for about two thirds of each day.
13. Add a hyphen.
    I took twenty seventh place in the race.
14. Circle the word that means involving the general public.
    The English civil war was fought to decide who should have the most power, the king or parliament.
15. The expression **armed to the teeth** means:
    ☐ completely armed.
    ☐ to chip a tooth.
16. The expression **to bite the dust** means:
    ☐ to be defeated.
    ☐ to act unfairly.
17. Circle two parts of the sentence joined by the conjunction.
    The king lost the seven-year war and his head.
18. Circle and write the verb group. _____
    For about ten years, Britain was ruled as a republic, not a monarchy.
19. The underlined word is: ☐ an adjective ☐ a verb
    After the death of the republican leader, the <u>defeated</u> king's son was crowned king.
20. Circle the conjunction.
    The new king was known as the 'merry monarch' because he focused on the joys of life.

MY SCORE

MY SCORE

UNIT 13

1. Circle the correct spelling.   transfussion   transfusion
2. Circle the incorrect spelling.   alternatively   alternativley
3. Circle the correct spelling.   politician   polititian
4. Circle the incorrect spelling.   efficiently   eficiently
5. A synonym for *artificial* is:
   ☐ articulate   ☐ synthetic   ☐ syringe
6. Use the prefixes *sub* and *super* to make two new words.
   charge _____   conscious _____
7. Write the plural or singular of each word.
   circle _____   deer _____
8. Circle the correct homophones.
   Rain is <u>dew/due</u> after the <u>dew/due</u> evaporates.
9. Count the syllables.   laminate ☐   lavender ☐
10. Write the adverb and noun from the adjective *perfect*.
    adverb _____   noun _____
11. Punctuate the sentence.
    the rabbit hops inside its cage when its feeling happy
12. Correct any punctuation errors.
    The animal's in the zoo were well nourished.
13. Add a full stop (**.**) question (**?**) or exclamation (**!**) mark.
    Watch out ☐ Didn't you see the bird flying at you ☐
14. Circle the verb written in the infinitive.
    To say that babies are born with no teeth is not quite true.
15. Circle and write the verb. _____
    Two sets of tooth buds lie hidden in a baby's gums.
16. Circle the adjectives.
    The visible, white part of the tooth is called the crown.
17. The underlined word is an: ☐ adjective ☐ adverb
    The roots of the tooth anchor it <u>firmly</u> in the jawbone.
18. Definite article. How many? ☐
    The white crown is a coating of hard enamel which covers the dentine layer of the exposed tooth.
19. Circle the word that means *soft and shapeless*.
    In the root, protected by the layer of dentine, is a pulpy mass of nerve endings and blood vessels.
20. Insert *is* or *are*.
    Children's milk teeth _____ replaced by permanent teeth as they get older.

1. Circle the incorrect spelling.   desperate   desparate
2. Circle the correct spelling.   perllution   pollution
3. Circle the incorrect spelling.   humilaty   humility
4. Circle the correct spelling.   insence   incense
5. An antonym for *generous* is:
   ☐ gracious   ☐ mayhem   ☐ meagre
6. Add the suffix *al* or *ous* to give the adjective.
   culture _____   torture _____
7. *provided* or *providing*? _____
   The man .... a new car to his wife on their anniversary.
8. The word *military* comes from the Latin word *militis*
   meaning ☐ dentist ☐ soldier
9. Listed alphabetically, the second word is _____.
   bizarre   bitumen   bistro   bivouac
10. Circle the word that does not belong in the word group.
    intense   intensify   intensity   intention
11. Add apostrophes as needed.
    Gregs and Beks bicycles were stolen yesterday.
12. How many guards? Add the apostrophe.
    ☐ one ☐ more than one
    This guards notebook was chewed by his dog.
13. Rewrite the phrase with an apostrophe.
    the wheels of the bicycle _____
14. Circle the prepositions.
    Before the Dark Ages, the people living in Ancient Greece came from different places and spoke their own languages.
15. Circle the verb group.
    During the Dark Ages, nothing was recorded.
16. Circle the word that means *small steps*.
    Travelling storytellers told tales in the Greek language and, gradually, everyone spoke Greek.
17. Circle the verb infinitive.
    Villages organised themselves into city-states which they worked together to defend.
18. This sentence is in the _____ tense.
    The people were loyal to their city-states rather than the land of Greece.
19. Circle the adverb.
    Each city-state was ruled independently.
20. Circle the proper nouns.
    Corinth was ruled by kings, Athens was ruled by an elected government and Sparta was ruled by a band of warriors.

MY SCORE

MY SCORE

UNIT 14

1. Circle the correct spelling. electricity electrisity
2. Circle the incorrect spelling. acquisition aquisition
3. Circle the correct spelling. respect respeckt
4. Circle the correct spelling. preseverence perseverance
5. A synonym for **barren** is:
   ◯ baron ◯ fertile ◯ infertile
6. Use the prefixes **sub** and **super** to make two new words.
   culture _____ glue _____
7. Write the plural or singular of each word.
   radius _____ teeth _____
8. Circle the correct homophones.
   The ceiling/sealing requires ceiling/sealing!
9. Count the syllables. magazine ◯ mandolin ◯
10. Write the adverb and noun from the adjective **angry**.
    adverb _____ noun _____
11. Punctuate the sentence.
    is it true that if you dont exercise your brain it will lose its ability to work properly
12. Are there any punctuation errors? ◯ yes ◯ no
    Dad still uses our dog's well-worn lead instead of her new one.
13. Add a full stop (**.**) question (**?**) or exclamation (**!**) mark.
    Taking a daily walk is good for you ◯ *Are you ready* ◯
14. Circle the proper nouns.
    The Masai people of Africa live in Kenya and Tanzania.
15. Circle the word that means **wandering from place to place**.
    The Masai are semi-nomadic, tribal people.
16. Circle the four prepositions.
    Masai live within fences built by the men with branches from the acacia tree.
17. Underline the verb.
    Women build loaf-shaped homes with sticks and mud.
18. Circle the feminine noun.
    Masai women and children shave their heads.
19. Circle the error.
    The Masai pierce there ears and wear colourful jewellery.
20. Insert **is** or **are**.
    Cattle, goats and sheep _____ important to the Masai economy.

1. Circle the incorrect spelling. bountiful bountyful
2. Circle the correct spelling. potencial potential
3. Circle the incorrect spelling. enthusiasm emfusiasm
4. Circle the correct spelling. miniature miniture
5. An antonym for **help** is:
   ◯ helm ◯ hind ◯ hinder
6. Add the suffix **al** or **ous** to give the adjective.
   adventure _____ nature _____
7. **their** or **they're** or **there**? _____
   I'm not sure where .... going.
8. Write an antonym of **minimum**. m_____
9. Listed alphabetically, the third word is _____ .
   discipline discomfort discourage disaster
10. Circle the word that does not belong in the word group.
    defence defend defensive deficient
11. Add possessive apostrophes as needed.
    Jill and Sandras favourite teacher taught history.
12. How many teachers? ◯ one ◯ more than one
    Add the apostrophe.
    That teachers lessons are always interesting.
13. Rewrite the phrase with an apostrophe.
    the lessons of some teachers
    _____
14. Circle the verb infinitive.
    Everyone has the right to be safe from all harm.
15. Write the pronoun. _____
    We should respect the rights of people.
16. This sentence is in the _____ tense.
    Sadly, many people do not respect the rights of others.
17. Insert **with** or **by**.
    In 1959, the 'Declaration of the rights of the child' was adopted _____ the United Nations.
18. **to** or **for**?
    The declaration includes ten rights relating _____ the special needs of children.
19. Circle the word meaning **simple**.
    In spite of this declaration, millions of children do not have basic human rights.
20. Circle the verb group.
    Throughout history, many people have been stripped of their human rights on a massive scale.

UNIT 14

MY SCORE

MY SCORE

DAY 135

1. Circle the correct spelling. handycraft handicraft
2. Circle the incorrect spelling. cisterm cistern
3. Circle the correct spelling. patiance patience
4. Circle the incorrect spelling. ecsept except
5. A synonym for **cautious** is:
    ☐ caustic ☐ careful ☐ careless
6. Use the prefixes **sub** and **super** to make two new words.
    division _____ grass _____
7. Write the plural or singular of each word.
    people _____
    child _____
8. Circle the correct homophones.
    In the old days, the made/maid had made/maid the fire before the family was up.
9. Count the syllables. negotiate ☐ nocturnal ☐
10. Write the adverb and noun from the adjective **certain**.
    adverb _____ noun _____
11. Punctuate the sentence.
    ive never watched that tv show is it any good
12. Correct any punctuation errors.
    I'd rather be active in my spare time than watch a screen, would'nt you!
13. Add a full stop (**.**) question (**?**) or exclamation (**!**) mark.
    You can't be active all the time ☐ *You must relax too* ☐
14. Circle the proper nouns.
    The Trans-Siberian Railway crosses Russia from Moscow in the west to Vladivostok in the east.
15. Insert **certainly** or **almost**.
    The railway line took _____ 15 years to complete.
16. Circle the prepositions.
    The line is over nine thousand kilometres long with 97 stops along the way.
17. Circle the infinitive of a verb.
    The journey takes at least six days to complete.
18. Circle the proper noun.
    For 200 km, the route hugs the shores of Lake Baikal.
19. The adjectives are ☐ comparative ☐ superlative.
    Lake Baikal is the oldest and deepest freshwater lake in the world.
20. The number **seven** is: ☐ an adjective.
    ☐ an adverb.
    The Trans-Siberian Railway crosses seven time zones.

DAY 136

1. Circle the incorrect spelling. guvernor governor
2. Circle the correct spelling. catastrophy catastrophe
3. Circle the incorrect spelling. reclaimable reclaimible
4. Circle the correct spelling. centenery centenary
5. An antonym for **hostile** is:
    ☐ fertile ☐ fiendish ☐ friendly
6. Add the suffix **al** or **ous** to give the adjective.
    humour _____ structure _____
7. **may** or **might**? _____
    I .... go to the beach if the weather stays calm.
8. Which word refers to a place?
    their they're there
9. Listed alphabetically, the last word is _____.
    galaxy gallant galleon galore
10. Circle the word that does not belong in the word group.
    satisfaction saturate satisfactorily satisfy
11. Add apostrophes as needed.
    Kanes and Abels homework was unfinished.
12. How many teachers? ☐ one ☐ more than one
    Add the apostrophe.
    Some teachers reactions are surprising.
13. Rewrite the phrase with an apostrophe.
    the homework of the senior pupils
    _____
14. Circle and write the proper adjective. _____
    Louis Pasteur was a 19th century French scientist.
15. Circle the present tense verb.
    Pasteur discovered that bacteria and germs cause disease.
16. Circle the word that means **carry** or **take**.
    Pasteur proved that bacteria can be transferred among people, animals and things.
17. Circle the indefinite article.
    Pasteur made a vaccine for preventing rabies, which was a common cause of death.
18. Circle the infinitive of a verb.
    Pasteur discovered that a yeast caused wine to go sour.
19. Circle the phrases connected by the conjunction.
    He found that heating the wine destroyed the yeast but did not damage the wine.
20. Circle the word that means **in its natural state**.
    This heating process is known as pasteurisation and it has been used to treat raw milk for about 150 years.

UNIT 14

1. Circle the correct spelling.   generosity   genorosity
2. Circle the incorrect spelling.   proportion   preportion
3. Circle the correct spelling.   certificate   cerstificate
4. Circle the incorrect spelling.   origernal   original
5. A synonym for **clarify** is:
   ☐ clarinet   ☐ explain   ☐ expose
6. Use the prefixes **sub** and **super** to make two new words.
   human _____   merge _____
7. Write the plural or singular of each word.
   fungi _____   tooth _____
8. Circle the correct homophones.
   The lessen/lesson on self-esteem helped to lessen/lesson the pressure some children felt.
9. Count the syllables.   omnivorous ☐ orchestra ☐
10. Write the adverb and noun from the adjective **hungry**.
    adverb _____   noun _____
11. Punctuate the sentence.
    i need to buy flour eggs dried fruit and sugar for the cake
12. Correct any punctuation errors.
    When separating eggs to make a meringue it's important that no yolk goes into the eggwhite.
13. Add a full stop (**.**) question (**?**) or exclamation (**!**) mark.
    What a delicious dessert ☐ How do you get it so crunchy ☐
14. Circle the proper noun.
    Napoleon Bonaparte was a famous French emperor.
15. Circle the proper adjective.
    While still a young man, Napoleon toppled the French government and became ruler of France.
16. Circle the word that means **huge**.
    In less than ten years, he had created a vast empire.
17. Circle the proper noun.
    His downfall came when he tried to invade Russia.
18. Circle the adjective.
    The soldiers were beaten by starvation and the bitter cold.
19. Circle the verb group.
    Napoleon was exiled to a Mediterranean island, but he escaped.
20. Circle the error.
    He was exiled again to an island in the South Atlantic Ocean where he died at the age in 52.

1. Circle the incorrect spelling.   circulation   circerlation
2. Circle the correct spelling.   paralise   paralyse
3. Circle the incorrect spelling.   replica   replicar
4. Circle the correct spelling.   fourfeit   forfeit
5. An antonym for **exit** is:
   ☐ entrance   ☐ impossible   ☐ important
6. Add the suffix **al** or **ous** to give the adjective.
   glamour _____
   horticulture _____
7. **moral** or **morale**? _____
   The players'......... improved when they finally won a match.
8. Circle the correct antonym for **polite**.
   inpolite   impolite
9. Listed alphabetically, the first word is _____.
   jaguar   jackal   jaffle   jacket
10. Circle the word that does not belong in the word group.
    friend   frieze   friendly   friendship
11. Add apostrophes as needed.
    Coco and Chanels puppies were born today.
12. How many puppies? ☐ one ☐ more than one
    Add the apostrophe.
    The puppies tails wagged wildly as they fed.
13. Rewrite the phrase with an apostrophe.
    two puppies of the dogs _____
14. Circle the nouns.
    An anaconda is a non-venomous, South American snake.
15. Circle and write the superlative adjective. _____
    The green anaconda is one of the world's largest snakes.
16. Which part of speech?   **live** ☐ noun ☐ verb
    lives ☐ noun ☐ verb
    Anacondas live solitary lives close to rivers and lakes.
17. Insert a suitable word.
    This giant snake can _____ to eight metres in length.
18. kg stands for _____
    At over 200 kg, the anaconda is a very heavy snake.
19. Circle the word that means offspring.
    The anaconda's young are born live, about 40 at a time.
20. Circle the reflexive pronoun.
    The anaconda kills its prey by wrapping itself around the body, causing suffocation.

MY SCORE

MY SCORE

DAY 139

1. Circle the correct spelling.   repertition   repetition

2. Circle the incorrect spelling. propeller   propellar

3. Circle the correct spelling. circumstance   circamstance

4. Circle the incorrect spelling. passidge   passage

5. A synonym for **deduct** is:
   ☐ dedicate   ☐ subtract   ☐ suppose

6. Use the prefixes **sub** and **super** to make two new words.
   power _____   title _____

7. Write the plural or singular of each word.
   people _____   uncle _____

8. Circle the correct homophones.
   The spectators were hoarse/horse from cheering at the closely fought hoarse/horse race.

9. Count the syllables.   papyrus ☐   precarious ☐

10. Write the adverb and noun from the adjective **spiteful**.
    adverb _____   noun _____

11. Punctuate the sentence.
    Ill buy my aunts present tomorrow she needs to check that its the right size

12. Correct any punctuation errors.
    Shopping with my aunts great fun because shes really quite eccentric.

13. Add a full stop (**.**) question (**?**) or exclamation (**!**) mark.
    See, I bought this ☐ Do you like it ☐

14. Circle the word that can also mean a small piece of land.
    Over 400 years ago, there was a plot to blow up the Houses of Parliament in London and kill the king.

15. The verb is in the: ☐ past tense   ☐ present tense.
    The king was making life very difficult for Roman Catholics to practise their faith.

16. Write one word to explain concealed. _____
    A group of men concealed barrels of gunpowder in the cellars.

17. Circle the verb infinitive.
    The plot was discovered and Guy Fawkes, who was about to light the explosives, was arrested.

18. Circle the two prepositions.
    Under torture, Guy Fawkes gave the names of the other men.

19. Circle the adjective intensifier.
    Guy Fawkes suffered a very grisly death.

20. Circle the verb group.
    Bonfires were lit across London to celebrate the king's lucky escape.

MY SCORE

DAY 140

1. Circle the incorrect spelling. painstakeing   painstaking

2. Circle the correct spelling.   fowndation   foundation

3. Circle the incorrect spelling. obedience   obediance

4. Circle the correct spelling.   procede   proceed

5. An antonym for **ferocious** is:
   ☐ fiendish   ☐ gentle   ☐ gigantic

6. Add the suffix **al** or **ous** to give the adjective.
   agriculture _____
   labour _____

7. **than** or **then**? _____
   An away win was more .... the team had hoped for.

8. The word **civilian** comes from the Latin word **civis** meaning: ☐ citizen   ☐ king

9. Listed alphabetically, the last word is _____.
   medicine   meddle   meditate   medallion

10. Circle the word that does not belong in the word group.
    necessary   necklace   necessarily   necessity

11. Add apostrophes as needed.
    Jacks and Jills best clothes were ruined.

12. How many farmers? ☐ one ☐ more than one
    Add the apostrophe.
    They had been climbing trees in that farmers garden.

13. Rewrite the phrase with an apostrophe.
    the property of all farmers
    _____

14. Insert **is** or **are**.
    Hieroglyphics _____ pictures that communicate a meaning.

15. The word **ancient** is: ☐ an adverb   ☐ an adjective
    The ancient Egyptians used over 700 hieroglyphics.

16. Circle the word that is not needed.
    For hundreds of years, no-one could not understand the hieroglyphics.

17. Circle the verb group.
    Then, in 1799, the Rosetta Stone was discovered.

18. Circle the conjunction.
    The stone was inscribed in Egyptian hieroglyphics and in Greek.

19. Circle the word that means **to decode**.
    Because the Greek could be read, the hieroglyphics could be deciphered and translated.

20. The word **by** is: ☐ a verb   ☐ a preposition
    Hieroglyphics were also used by the Maya and Aztec indians of Central America.

MY SCORE

1. Which is correct?   orgernisation   organisation

2. Which is incorrect?   variation   vairiation

3. Which is correct?   confidance   confidence

4. Which is incorrect?   erosion   errosion

5. A synonym for **detach** is:

   ☐ detect   ☐ separate   ☐ sequence

6. Use the prefixes **post** and **pre** to make two new words.

   date _____   mature _____

7. Write the plural or singular of each word.

   oxen _____   sheep _____

8. Circle the correct homophones.

   He used time/thyme the last time/thyme he cooked pasta.

9. Count the syllables.   qualify ☐   quantify ☐

10. Write the adverb and noun from the adjective **miserable**.

    adverb _____   noun _____

11. Add commas to the sentence.

    Ingredients include dried fruit nuts and seeds wheat bran and oat flakes.

12. Correct any punctuation errors.

    do we have to toast the flakes first

13. Punctuate.

    Heat the honey and butter first instructed Mum.

14. Insert **behind** or **under.**

    The USSR was a group of countries that were

    joined as one state _____ communist rule.

15. Circle the verb.

    The union existed for about 70 years from 1922 until 1991.

16. The adjective is: ☐ comparative ☐ superlative

    Russia was the largest country in the union, in area and in population.

17. The verb group is: ☐ present tense ☐ past tense

    The politics and economy of the USSR, also known as the Soviet Union, were dominated by Russia.

18. Circle the prepositions.

    The people of the USSR were controlled by the state in all areas of their daily lives.

19. Circle the word meaning **important**.

    After World War II, the USSR became a major world power.

20. Circle the meaning closest to **clash**.

    The USSR and the USA had many political differences; this conflict was called the Cold War.

1. Which is correct?   abominable   abominible

2. Which is correct?   perpendicular   perpendicula

3. Which is incorrect? estuery   estuary

4. Which is incorrect? corosion   corrosion

5. An antonym for **meagre** is:

   ☐ miserable   ☐ abolish   ☐ abundant

6. Add the suffix **tious** to give the adjective.

   caution _____

7. **personal** or **personnel**? _____

   All .... in the office deserved a pay increase.

8. The word **lunar** comes from the Latin word **luna** meaning: ☐ moon   ☐ water

9. Listed alphabetically, the first word is _____.

   capsize   capacity   captive   capital

10. Circle the word that does not belong in the word group.

    intend   intensity   intention   intentionally

11. Insert the missing punctuation mark.

    What is the time ☐

12. Insert the missing punctuation mark.

    Look at the time ☐

13. Insert the missing punctuation mark.

    Today is the day after yesterday ☐

14. **is** or **are**?

    In the USA, there _____ two main political parties, the Democratic Party and the Republican Party.

15. Circle the opposite of **weak**.

    Democrats believe the federal government should have a strong influence on the whole country.

16. The adjective is: ☐ comparative ☐ superlative

    Republicans believe individuals and communities should have a stronger voice.

17. There are ☐ definite articles in this sentence.

    The symbol for the Democratic Party is the donkey and for the Republican Party, the elephant.

18. Is the verb group underlined? ☐ yes ☐ no

    The Democratic Party was established in 1824, the Republican Party 30 years later, in 1854.

19. Circle the infinitive form of a verb.

    Abraham Lincoln was the first Republican president and, in 1865, the first to be assassinated.

20. Circle the superlative adjective.

    Three other presidents have been assassinated, the most recent being John F Kennedy, who was shot in 1963.

MY SCORE   MY SCORE

1. Which is correct? conserquently consequently
2. Which is incorrect? punctuality puncshuality
3. Which is correct? electrition electrician
4. Which is incorrect? melodious melodius
5. A synonym for **dubious** is:
   ☐ doubtful ☐ dour ☐ drab
6. Use the prefixes **post** and **pre** to make two new words.
   caution _____ graduate _____
7. Write the plural or singular of each word.
   gas _____ offspring _____
8. Circle the correct homophones.
   You might not find a cool desert/dessert in the scorching desert/dessert.
9. Count the syllables. reaction ☐ recuperate ☐
10. Write the adverb and noun from the adjective **proud**.
    adverb _____ noun _____
11. Add commas to the sentence.
    At the end of World War II women who had been working in jobs traditionally done by men had to give up their work.
12. Correct any punctuation errors.
    Women liked being paid to work so they found jobs elsewhere
13. Punctuate.
    Why were women not paid equally enquired the child
14. Circle the proper nouns.
    Mao Zedong was a founder of the Chinese Communist Party.
15. Circle the conjunction.
    When the Communist Party took control of the country, the People's Republic of China was born.
16. Circle the proper adjective.
    Chairman Mao wanted to reshape Chinese society according to his version of communism, Maoism.
17. Correct the error.
    To begin with, Mao recieved help from the USSR.
18. Circle the adverb.
    Mao's attempts to create a better China involved massive changes that occurred quickly.
19. Circle two conjunctions.
    Millions died in famines when harvests failed and more lost their lives by opposing Mao's authority.
20. One word that means the same as **harsh** is _____.
    Many Westerners believe he was a harsh leader, but many in China think he was a great ruler.

MY SCORE

1. Which is incorrect? dissern discern
2. Which is correct? pityful pitiful
3. Which is incorrect? circit circuit
4. Which is correct? literate litterate
5. An antonym for **genuine** is:
   ☐ mean ☐ friendly ☐ fake
6. Add the suffix **cious** or **tious** to give the adjective.
   ambition _____ atrocity _____
7. **exterior** or **interior**? _____
   The .... of the house was filled with valuable paintings and furniture.
8. The word **gem** comes from the Latin word **gemma** meaning: ☐ genie ☐ jewel
9. Listed alphabetically, the last word is _____.
   enigma enough engrave engulf
10. Circle the word that does not belong in the word group.
    object oblige objective objectively
11. Insert the missing punctuation mark.
    'Oh no, it's raining ☐' cried Anna.
12. Insert the missing punctuation mark.
    I love autumn ☐ it's my favourite season.
13. Insert the missing punctuation mark.
    As the wind howled ☐ we kept warm by the fire.
14. Circle the proper adjective.
    Why does nobody expect the Spanish Inquisition?
15. Circle the word meaning **belief(s)**.
    For 350 years, the Spanish Inquisition travelled the country in search of anyone who did not support the Catholic faith.
16. Which word has two different meanings?
    So they could rule without opposition, the king and queen of Spain wanted all their subjects to be Catholics.
17. The underlined word is a _____.
    People who were not Catholics lived in fear of being discovered by the Spanish Inquisition.
18. Circle the adverb.
    The Spanish immediately arrested anyone suspected of being a non-believer.
19. Finish the word.
    The inquisition was ruthless and cr_____.
20. Write a homophone of one of the words. _____
    Many people were imprisoned or publicly executed under the Spanish Inquisition's reign of terror.

MY SCORE

UNIT 15

DAY 145

1. Which is correct?   deceit   deciet

2. Which is incorrect?   alternately   allternately

3. Which is correct?   honesty   honersty

4. Which is incorrect?   reclaimation   reclamation

5. A synonym for **magnify** is:
   ☐ magnet   ☐ enlarge   ☐ endure

6. Use the prefixes **post** and **pre** to make two new words.
   history _____   mortem _____

7. Write the plural or singular of each word.
   criteria _____   tableaux _____

8. Circle the correct homophones.
   He had to sow/sew/so his shirt sow/sew/so he could go out and sow/sew/so the grass seeds.

9. Count the syllables.   sacrifice ☐   sediment ☐

10. Write the adverb and noun from the adjective **grateful**.
    adverb _____   noun _____

11. Punctuate the sentence.
    one of the most successful kings in europe in the first century ad was charlemagne king of the franks

12. Correct any punctuation errors in the sentence.
    charlemagne was known as charles the great

13. Punctuate.
    i read about charles in my book History of Europe

14. Circle the proper adjective.
    The British naval officer, Robert Falcon Scott, is better known as 'Scott of the Antarctic'.

15. Circle the conjunction.
    After leading a successful expedition to the Antarctic, Scott wanted to reach the South Pole.

16. Circle the conjunction.
    The fateful expedition began with teams of sleds, ponies and donkeys, but they were overcome by the terrible conditions.

17. Circle the two verb infinitives.
    The men continued on foot and managed to reach the pole only to find a Norwegian flag flying there.

18. Circle the plural noun.
    Disappointed, the men began the journey home.

19. Circle the pronoun.
    They were suffering from frostbite and starvation.

20. Insert a suitable word.
    The explorers never completed their return _____ .

MY SCORE

DAY 146

1. Which is correct?   demonstration   demonstrateion

2. Which is correct?   circumfrence   circumference

3. Which is incorrect?   loyalty   loyerlty

4. Which is correct?   responsibility   responsability

5. An antonym for **vague** is:
   ☐ vogue   ☐ deliberate   ☐ definite

6. Add the suffix **cious** or **tious** to give the adjective.
   infection _____   pretension _____

7. **permanent** or **temporary**? _____
   That stain will never come out so it will be ....

8. The word **solar** comes from the Latin word **sola**
   meaning: ☐ sun   ☐ soul

9. Listed alphabetically, the third word is _____ .
   hostel   hostage   hostile   hospital

10. Circle the word that does not belong in the word group.
    reason   reasonable   reassure   reasonably

11. Insert the missing punctuation marks.
    Jai spoke excitedly ☐☐ Who's turn is it next?'

12. Insert the missing punctuation mark.
    Jai ☐s uncle had given him a new board game.

13. Insert the missing punctuation mark.
    Jai received board games ☐ DVDs, books and much more for his birthday.

14. Circle the pronoun and the noun it refers to.
    Before Russia became a part of the Soviet Union, it was a monarchy ruled by Russian tsars.

15. Circle the verb.
    The Romanov family ruled the empire for about 300 years.

16. Circle the verb group.
    Queen Victoria's granddaughter, Alexandra, was married to the last Emperor of Russia, Tsar Nicholas II.

17. Circle the definite article.
    During World War I, the people of Russia turned against the royal family.

18. **Visitor** has: ☐ masculine gender.
                        ☐ common gender.
    The family were held under house arrest for over a year and no visitor was allowed there.

19. Circle the collective noun.
    In July 1918, the family were assassinated by soldiers of the revolutionary army.

20. Circle the adjective.
    The history of Russia is interesting.

MY SCORE

1. Which is correct?   manyerscript   manuscript

2. Which is incorrect?   centigrade   centergrade

3. Which is correct?   reverlution   revolution

4. Which is incorrect?   assistant   asisstant

5. A synonym for *entire* is:
   ☐ entice   ☐ complete   ☐ commence

6. Use the prefixes *post* and *pre* to make two new words.

   haste _____   judge _____

7. Write the plural or singular of each word.

   radius _____   analysis _____

8. Circle the correct homophones.

   I wood/would prefer my furniture to be made of wood/
   would rather than laminate.

9. Count the syllables.   technology ☐   tragedy ☐

10. Write the adverb and noun from the adjective *humble*.

    adverb _____   noun _____

11. Punctuate the sentence.

    although the united kingdom is densely populated it
    does have many country areas.

12. Correct any punctuation errors in the sentence.

    For many people walking in the countryside is a favourite
    pastime; there are many walking trails.

13. Punctuate.

    there are beautiful mountains and lakes in Ireland
    observed the tourist

14. Insert a suitable word.

    After the Great Plague killed so many people in

    London, the city was _____ by a fire.

15. Circle the conjunction.

    Most of the buildings in London were made of wood so
    the fire spread easily.

16. Circle the noun that *it* refers to.

    Although the fire brought problems, it destroyed the filthy
    areas that had helped the plague spread.

17. Circle the masculine noun.

    The fire began in Pudding Lane in the shop owned by
    the King's baker.

18. Circle the word meaning *to make certain*.

    The maid who did not ensure the ovens were put out
    properly was one of the few casualties of the fire.

19. Circle the word meaning *escaped*.

    Although he had fled to the countryside during the
    plague, the king stayed in London during the fire.

20. Circle the conjunction.

    The fire died when the wind blew the flames back over
    the city.

MY SCORE

1. Which is incorrect?   redugtion   reduction

2. Which is correct?   prercaution   precaution

3. Which is incorrect?   misstaken   mistaken

4. Which is correct?   oppersition   opposition

5. An antonym for *certain* is:
   ☐ dubious   ☐ certify   ☐ definite

6. Add the suffix *cious* or *tious* to give the adjective.

   malice _____   nutrition _____

7. *exterior* or *interior*? _____
   Thankfully, the rain only damaged the .... of the house.

8. The word *stellar* comes from the Latin word *stella*
   meaning   ☐ moon   ☐ star

9. Listed alphabetically, the second word is _____ .
   kindle   kitchen   kidnap   kiln

10. Circle the word that does not belong in the word group.
    safari   safe   safely   safety

11. Insert the missing punctuation mark.

    The Rosetta Stone helped historians solve the
    hieroglyphic symbols ☐

12. Insert one punctuation mark.

    The study of ancient cultures, such as the Chinese the
    Greeks and the Maya, reveals a lot about our past.

13. Insert the missing punctuation mark.

    Many things were developed in ancient times: the
    wheel, paper, irrigation and central heating

14. The sentence is the _____ tense.
    Caligula was a Roman emperor known for his wild
    behaviour.

15. Circle the indefinite article.
    One of his most famous stunts was to ride his horse
    across a stretch of the Bay of Naples.

16. Circle the opposite of permanent.
    To perform this stunt, he built a temporary bridge.

17. Circle the verb written in the infinite.
    Boats were tied together to form a floating platform.

18. Circle the two verbs.
    Dressed in fine armour, Caligula charged across the bay
    on horseback.

19. Circle the preposition.
    The next day, Caligula made the return journey on a
    chariot.

20. Circle the verb group.
    Caligula was assassinated after only four years as
    emperor.

MY SCORE

UNIT 15

DAY 149

1. Which is correct?   percieve   perceive

2. Which is incorrect?   believible   believable

3. Which is correct?   constitution   constitusion

4. Which is incorrect?   optimism   optermism

5. A synonym for **humiliate** is:
   ☐ humility   ☐ embrace   ☐ embarrass

6. Use the prefixes **post** and **pre** to make two new words.
   meditate _____   script _____

7. Write the plural or singular of each word.
   government _____   salmon _____

8. Circle the correct homophones.
   As the war/wore war/wore on, millions were killed.

9. Count the syllables.   ventilate ☐   versatile ☐

10. Write the adverb and noun from the adjective **desperate**.
    adverb _____   noun _____

11. Punctuate the sentence.
    The 72 year reign of Louis XIV of France began in the second half of the 17th century

12. Correct any punctuation errors in the sentence.
    Louis was known as the sun king believing himself to be the sun and his subjects the planets.

13. Punctuate.
    did you know that france became a very powerful European country explained the historian.

14. **its** or **it's**?
    Towards the end of World War II, Japan realised it was struggling against _____ opposition forces.

15. Circle the masculine noun.
    The emperor created a special attack unit.

16. Circle the plural nouns.
    The kamikaze pilots were suicide bombers who flew their planes into enemy ships.

17. Circle the collective noun.
    Kamikaze, meaning divine wind, was the name given to a typhoon that destroyed an enemy fleet.

18. Circle the conjunction.
    Most pilots joined the kamikaze unit so they would not bring shame to their families.

19. Circle the word meaning **symbol**.
    Each pilot wore a headband embroidered with the rising sun emblem.

20. Insert a suitable noun.
    After they took-off, _____ dropped flowers onto a holy mountain before heading to their mission and certain death.

DAY 150

1. Which is incorrect?   desicive   decisive

2. Which is correct?   electracute   electrocute

3. Which is incorrect?   determenation   determination

4. Which is correct?   enjoyment   enjoymment

5. An antonym for **fragile** is:
   ☐ flimsy   ☐ strength   ☐ strong

6. Add the suffix **cious** or **tious** to give the adjective.
   conscience _____   vivacity _____

7. **bough** or **bow**? _____
   It is a sign of respect when people ....

8. Circle the word which relates to the moon.
   stellar   lunar   solar

9. Listed alphabetically, the first word is _____.
   nation   nature   native   natural

10. Circle the word that does not belong in the word group.
    responsible   respire   responsibly   responsive

11. Insert the missing punctuation mark.
    As Theo carefully lifted the lid of the old box ☐ the cat screeched and ran out of the room.

12. Insert the missing punctuation mark.
    'Look at him go ☐' gasped Theo to himself.

13. Insert the missing punctuation mark.
    'Whatever made him react like that ☐'

14. Write **of** or **in**.
    Earth has always had its force _____ gravity.

15. Circle one infinitive verb.
    Isaac Newton was the first to realise gravity existed when he was struck by an apple while sitting under an apple tree.

16. Circle the past tense verb group.
    Newton had been exploring how things moved.

17. **objects** or **subjects**? _____
    Newton studied the effects of gravity on .... of different mass falling from different heights.

18. Write 16th in words. _____
    Many discoveries had been made in the 16th century.

19. **is** or **are**?
    Newton developed many scientific laws which _____ still used today.

20. Insert a suitable word.
    Newton proved that the sun, not Earth, is the centre of the solar _____ .

MY SCORE

MY SCORE

REVISION DAYS 1–10

1. Correct the spelling mistake. _____
   Raise your hand if you know the anzer.

2. Circle the correct spelling.   ocassion   occasion

3. Correct the spelling mistake. _____
   I am not userly late for school.

4. Circle the correct spelling.   vareius   various

5. A synonym for **entangled** is:
   ☐ caught   ☐ released   ☐ hidden

6. Add a prefix to give the opposite meaning.
   _____agree   _____mortal

7. Write as a contraction.
   might have _____

8. Write the homophone of **flour**. _____

9. Circle the word with a different number of syllables.
   bicycle   calendar   certain

10. Write the plural of **church**. _____

11. Add commas.
    One day you will like carrots peas beans and onion.

12. Add speech marks to show what was said.
    Please, may I have some more? asked Oliver.

13. Add an apostrophe.
    The churches spires were silhouetted against the sky.

14. Circle the proper nouns.
    The acting agency asked Brett and Joli to work again.

15. Circle the adjectives.
    Joli is beautiful, tall and French but also rather rude.

16. Past, present or future tense? _____
    Rehearsals for the play will begin in one week.

17. **Adverb** or **preposition**? _____
    With grace and glamour, Joli swept on to the stage.

18. Circle and write the collective noun. _____
    The cast included local men and women.

19. Comparative or superlative? _____
    Joli was the most famous, but not the best actor.

20. Circle the negative verb.
    Joli was not pleased by the audience response.

21. Correct the spelling mistake. _____
    The libery closed early today.

22. Circle the correct spelling.   surprise   suprise

23. Rearrange the letters to make a word that means **move out of sight**.
    aadeipprs _____

24. Correct the spelling mistake. _____
    I will probbly go to the shops tomorrow.

25. An antonym for **doubtful** is: _____
    certain   unlikely   impossible

26. Add the suffix that means **without**.
    sense_____   fear_____

27. Write **allowed** and **aloud** in the correct places.
    You are not _____ to read _____ in silent reading.

28. Write a synonym for **brave**.   c_____

29. In the dictionary, **engrave** comes before _____.
    engine   engulf   enforce

30. Which word does not have an **oa** (**boat**) sound?
    toe   boast   now   globe

31. Complete the punctuation.
    You will do as I say, Cotter! exploded Professor Drape

32. Add a comma to the statement.
    Although I am young I have travelled a great deal.

33. Add apostrophes.
    Mums parents.

34. Circle the adverb.
    To our surprise, the train arrived early.

35. Circle three nouns.
    All the traffic at the station made the air smell awful.

36. Choose the phrase.   ☐ less busy   ☐ less busier
    The station is .... during the day than in the morning or evening.

37. Add the verb.   walk   walks   walked
    Always _____ through the ticket barrier on the left.

38. Circle the verb group.
    The train will leave promptly at 3.15 pm.

39. Add the verb.   catched   caught   caughted
    I would have _____ the earlier train but I was late.

40. Circle the proper nouns.
    The train stopped at Usk, Gar and all stations to Chestle.

MY SCORE

1. Correct the spelling mistake. _____

   I hardly reconise the house since it's been renovated.

2. Circle the correct spelling.   neusanse   nuisance

3. Correct the spelling mistake. _____

   The house will be avaylable to rent for the holidays.

4. Circle the correct spelling.   perswaid   persuade

5. A synonym for **frequently** is:

   ☐ never   ☐ often   ☐ seldom

6. Add a prefix to give each word the opposite meaning.

   _____respect   _____qualify

7. Write as a contraction.

   would have   _____

8. Write the homophone of **bored**. _____

9. Separate **necessary** into its syllables. _____

10. The plural of **radio** is _____.

11. Add three types of punctuation mark.

    Gary cried out Watch out Tom It's Lord Walbernort

12. Add the apostrophe.

    Lord Walbernort heard Garys screams.

13. Add the commas.

    Gary Tom Germaine and Hidreg stood still.

14. Circle the common noun.

    Slowly, Lord Walbernort approached the four friends.

15. Circle the pronoun.

    With a flash of magic, they were rescued on a flying carpet.

16. Circle the adjectives.

    The air was warm and comforting.

17. Adverb or preposition? _____

    The children arrived promptly at the school.

18. Circle the definite article.

    Walking up to school, the friends remained calm.

19. Write the preposition. _____

    Standing beneath the arch, they knew they were safe.

20. Write the conjunction. _____

    Feeling rather strange and very tired, they decided to go straight to bed.

21. Correct the spelling mistake. _____

    Slugs can easily damidge your garden plants.

22. Circle the correct spelling.   excllent   excellent

23. Correct the spelling mistake. _____

    I am defernate that I did not take your book.

24. Circle the correct spelling.   hieght   height

25. An antonym for **relaxed** is:

    ☐ difficult   ☐ stressed   ☐ strange

26. Add the suffix **ous** and write the adjective.

    fame _____   glory _____

27. Write **stairs** or **stares** in the sentence.

    The new house still has no _____ in it.

28. Write a synonym for **sly**.   c_____

29. In the dictionary, _____ comes before **surly**.

    surprise   surge   survive

30. Circle the word that does not have a silent letter.

    sword   knight   chest   wrong

31. Add capital letters.

    anna lived on the mountain with grandpa joel.

32. Add the missing comma.

    Every spring Anna took the goats to the high pasture.

33. Circle the simile.

    Anna felt as safe as houses living with her grandpa.

34. Circle the proper nouns.

    Anna and Joel cared for Peter during the storm.

35. Tick.   ☐ adjective   ☐ abstract noun

    For Peter, it was a true <u>delight</u> to look after the village goats.

36. Proper noun or proper adjective? _____

    Life in the <u>Swiss</u> Alps was wonderful for Anna.

37. Circle the verb group.

    Grandpa had lived in the Alps for many years.

38. Circle and write the preposition. _____

    One day, Joel's sister came to take Anna to the city.

39. **too** or **to**?

    Anna did not want _____ leave with her great-aunt.

40. Write the conjunction. _____

    She left her beloved mountains and lived in a grey city.

MY SCORE

1. Correct the spelling mistake. _____

   To acheive a good result, you must work hard.

2. Circle the correct spelling. enuff enough

3. Correct the spelling mistake. _____

   I am certin I locked the door this morning.

4. Circle the correct spelling. learn lurn

5. A synonym for **erase** is:

   ☐ hide ☐ delete ☐ capture

6. Add the prefix **in** or **il** to give the opposite meaning.

   _____legible _____adequate

7. Write as a contraction.

   will not _____

8. Write the correct homophone. _____

   It was a long walk for the bride and her father to the altar/alter.

9. Separate **desperate** into its syllables. _____

10. The singular of **diaries** is _____ .

11. Add a comma to give the sentence sense.

    Although Dad could eat the problem still bothered him.

12. Add a comma.

    Because he needs a lot of work done Dad has to visit the dentist.

13. Add commas to the list.

    Dad's other problems include: a bad back sore knees rickety hips ingrown toenails and bunions.

14. Write the common noun. _____

    The race starts at the beginning of July.

15. Circle the proper adjective.

    This famous annual race is challenging and was won by a Scottish driver.

16. Circle the proper nouns.

    The annual race around France always ends in Paris.

17. Write the comparative adjective. _____

    The race in France is longer than the one in Italy.

18. Write the superlative adjective. _____

    Of the three races, in Italy, France and Spain, the one in France is the most famous.

19. Circle the word that does not belong.

    My dream holiday would be to follow the French race there.

20. Write the pronouns. _____

    We all have dream holidays—what's yours?

21. Correct the spelling mistake. _____

    Tennis is the most populur sport in our class.

22. Circle the correct spelling. favourite favrit

23. Correct the spelling mistake. _____

    My dad will be fourty next year.

24. Circle the correct spelling. disastrus disastrous

25. An antonym for **deny** is:

    ☐ truth ☐ believe ☐ admit

26. Write the adjective made when the suffix **ous** is added to the nouns.

    mountain_____ ridicule_____

27. Write **expand** or **contract**.

    If things shrink and shorten, we say they

    _____ .

28. Write a synonym for **enemy**. f_____

29. In the dictionary, _____ precedes **paradise**.

    parallel paralysed parachute

30. In which word is the letter **k** silent?

    ☐ duck ☐ khaki ☐ knowledge

31. Add an apostrophe.

    Jans visits to the library became less frequent.

32. Complete the simile.

    as neat as a _____

33. Add an apostrophe.

    The womens changing room is next to the stairs.

34. Another verb for **said**. _____

    The man said, 'The show is about to begin.'

35. Write the missing word.

    a _____ of lions

36. Circle the verb group.

    I would prefer to relax in the sunshine.

37. Circle the adverb.

    We won't walk quickly, so you'll be able to keep up.

38. Write the adverb that tells **when**. _____

    I saw this programme before.

39. Circle the preposition.

    We'll walk to the old bridge.

40. Write the conjunction. _____

    When you are fitter, we'll be able to walk further.

MY SCORE

1. Correct the spelling mistake. _____

   My favourite carachter in the story is Billy Bob McGee.

2. Circle the correct spelling.   especially   espeshlly

3. Correct the spelling mistake. _____

   Twelthf night is a comedy play by William Shakespeare.

4. Circle the correct spelling.   wierd   weird

5. A synonym for **curious** is:

   ☐ wild   ☐ inquisitive   ☐ wonderful

6. Add the prefix **dis** to give the opposite meaning.

   _____agree   _____obey

7. Expand.

   shan't _____

8. Write the correct homophone. _____

   As I wandered/wondered along the path, I thought of you.

9. Separate **privilege** into its syllables. _____

10. The plural of **sky** is _____ .

11. Rewrite the phrase using an apostrophe.
    the branches of the trees

    _____

12. Circle the sentence that requires speech marks.

    Where are you going? asked Dad.

    Dad asked me where I was going.

13. Which word means **to knock down**?

    demolish   deter

14. Circle the preposition.

    I had left Dad's present in the shed.

15. Circle the conjunction.

    I wanted to get it but now I would have to wait.

16. Preposition or conjunction? _____

    I will sneak it in through the window.

17. Circle the definite article.

    The new racing bike was hidden under a blanket.

18. Circle the indefinite article.

    Dad had wanted a new bike for so long.

19. Circle the adjectives.

    Dad will love the shiny, new bike we got him.

20. Circle the verb.

    Dad was in for the most amazing birthday treat!

21. Correct the spelling mistake. _____

    There is beutty all around us.

22. Circle the correct spelling.   curiousity   curiosity

23. Correct the spelling mistake. _____

    My dad can embarass me when he dances.

24. Circle the correct spelling.   rhythm   rhythum

25. An antonym for **conceited** is:

    ☐ conscious   ☐ haughty   ☐ humble

26. Write the adjective made when the suffix **al** is added to the nouns.

    logic _____   music _____

27. **cells** or **sells**? _____

    Our bodies are composed of millions of ....

28. Write an antonym for **import**.   e_____

29. Alphabetically, which word precedes **throne**?

    through   throat   throttle

30. Circle the compound word that needs a hyphen.

    sixteen   nineteen   thirtythree

31. How many owners?   ☐ one   ☐ more than one

    the senior schools' pupils

32. Circle the direct speech.

    Troy groaned loudly, Isn't dinner ready yet?

33. Which word means to think about something?

    chaos   contemplate   contempt

34. Circle the pronoun.

    Troy helped his mum prepare dinner so it would be ready sooner.

35. Circle the conjunction.

    His stomach rumbled as he set the table.

36. Pronoun or adjective? _____

    Troy thinks his mum's cooking is the best there is.

37. Circle the correct part.

    For years, Troy has/is helped his mum in the kitchen.

38. Circle the correct verb.

    Troy's mum is/has always giving him cooking tips.

39. Tick.   ☐ conjunction
           ☐ preposition

    Troy has always been a great help in the house.

40. Circle the word that is not needed.
    Troy also likes to help his dad in the intense garden.

MY SCORE

1. Circle the word spelt incorrectly.   bizness   business

2. Rewrite the incorrectly spelt word. _____

   coastal   tempriture   vegetable

3. Circle the correct spelling.   language   langwidge

4. Rewrite the word spelt incorrectly. _____

   natural   mention   diserbilerty

5. A synonym for **hazardous** is:

   ☐ dangerous   ☐ haphazard   ☐ delightful

6. In which word are the letters **fore** not a prefix meaning **before**?

   foreign   forehead   forefinger

7. The contraction in **what'd happened** means _____ .

8. Circle the correct homophone.

   I enjoyed watching the cereal/serial on television.

9. The syllables of **disastrous** are _____ .

10. Write the plural of each noun.

    torch _____   echo _____

    patio _____

11. Add the apostrophe.

    All the spectators cries were heard across the park.

12. Circle the direct speech.

    Come on, Falcons! wailed Tom, Don't let them win!

13. Add speech marks to show the direct speech.

    My team, announced Tom proudly, won the championship.

14. Circle the verbs.

    In the late 1800s, the Wright brothers owned a bicycle shop where they sold models they had designed themselves.

15. Circle the conjunction.

    Although they were successful, they had a greater vision.

16. **gestures** or **techniques**?

    The brothers used many _____ to build a full-sized flying machine.

17. Circle the definite article.

    The brothers tossed a coin to see who would pilot the machine's maiden flight.

18. Circle the verb.

    That first flight lasted just 12 seconds.

19. Finish the proverb.

    _____ *flock together.*

20. Finish the proverb.

    _____ *that ends well.*

21. Circle the word spelt correctly.   ernuff   enough

22. Rewrite the incorrectly spelt word. _____

    sincearly   energy   strength

23. Circle the incorrect spelling. oppertunity opportunity

24. Rewrite the incorrectly spelt word. _____

    physical   relavant   knowledge

25. An antonym for **serious** is: ☐ severe ☐ hilarious

26. Add the suffix **ly** to these words.

    dangerous _____

    wicked _____

27. **main** or **mane**? _____

    I can't find the .... entrance.

28. Write a synonym for **exterior**.   o_____

29. Alphabetically, _____ precedes **beard**.

    beast   beauty   beacon

30. Which pair of words forms a compound word?

    walking stick   riding boots   rain forest

31. How many owners? ☐ one ☐ more than one

    the jockeys' riding silks

32. Add speech marks.

    This race, began the trainer, is the last of the season.

33. Add speech marks to show the direct speech.

    This evening, he continued, we will celebrate our success.

34. **provoked** or **renowned**?

    The Bermuda Triangle is _____ .

35. Write the plural nouns.

    _____   _____

    Ships and planes mysteriously disappeared here.

36. Write **is** or **are**.

    Scientists believe the incidents that have occurred _____ the result of human error and weather conditions.

37. Circle the preposition.

    Many ships and planes regularly travel across the Bermuda Triangle without incident.

38. Circle the error.

    Some people even beleave that supernatural forces are responsible for the strange event.

39. Circle the conjunction.

    The legend of the Bermuda Triangle began when stories of the disappearances reached the public.

40. Finish the proverb.

    _____ *has a silver lining.*

MY SCORE

1. Correct the spelling.   flexable   _____

2. Correct the spelling.   imaganation   _____

3. Correct the spelling.   untill   _____

4. Correct the spelling.   sissors   _____

5. A synonym for **sleeping** is:
   ☐ lazy   ☐ dormant   ☐ slothful

6. The letters **mis** are a prefix meaning **wrongly** in:
   ☐ mischief   ☐ misfortune   ☐ mislaid

7. The contraction in **Dad's going too** means _____ .

8. Circle the correct homophone.
   The main <u>coarse/course</u> of the meal was delicious.

9. Circle the word with more syllables.   curious   precious

10. Add **ed** to give the past participle of each verb.
    cry _____   try _____
    fry _____

11. There: ☐ are two sentences.
           ☐ is one sentence.
    'After lunch', said Dad, 'we'll all go to the beach'.

12. The underlined is followed by a:
    ☐ comma. ☐ full stop.
    'If you're lucky', <u>he added</u>, 'there'll be plenty of waves'.

13. Add a full stop or comma.
    'Maybe', he continued ☐ 'some of your friends will be there'.

14. Circle the preposition.
    The Inca Empire came to an end in a small room which is known as 'the ransom room'.

15. Circle the plural noun.
    The Inca emperor was arrested for crimes against Spain and he was burned at the stake.

16. Circle the error.
    Atahuallpa offered as much gold and silver as would fill his prison sell so that his life would be spared.

17. Circle the proper noun.
    If he converted to their religion, the Spanish promised that Atahuallpa would not die by fire.

18. Circle the word that is not needed.
    Even though Atahuallpa agreed that and became a Catholic, his life was not spared.

19. Insert a suitable noun.
    Before his _____ was thrown on the fire, Atahuallpa was strangled.

20. Which expression means **not to take sides in an argument**.
    ☐ in the same boat   ☐ sit on the fence

21. Correct the spelling.   eigtht   _____

22. Correct the spelling.   straihgt   _____

23. Correct the spelling.   derlightful   _____

24. Correct the spelling.   viserble   _____

25. Circle an antonym for **compulsory**. optional definitely

26. Add the suffixes **ment** or **ful** to these words.
    wonder _____
    enjoy _____

27. Write **its** or **it's**.
    When ____ hungry, the dog eats from ____ bowl.

28. The word **liberty** comes from the Latin word **libera** meaning: ☐ free   ☐ library

29. Listed alphabetically, the first word is _____ .
    servant   serious   serpent   series

30. Which word does not belong in the group?
    zebra   tiger   lion   panther

31. There: ☐ are two sentences.
           ☐ is one sentence.
    'You have done well this season', said the coach. 'You deserve to be at the top of the league.'

32. The underlined is followed by a: ☐ capital.
                                      ☐ lower-case letter.
    'You will need to keep active during the break', <u>she added</u>. 'You could try playing a different sport.'

33. Add a **capital** or a **lower-case i**.
    'Swimming is a good choice', she continued. ☐t can keep you fit without the risk of injuries!'

34. Circle the proper noun.
    Many people believe that Timbuktu exists only in legends.

35. Circle the preposition.
    But Timbuktu is located in Mali, West Africa.

36. Circle the conjunction.
    Timbuktu was a wealthy city and major trading centre.

37. Circle the verb group.
    For years, European explorers had failed to find Timbuktu.

38. Which word means **to shrink gradually**.
    ☐ dwindle   ☐ scant

39. Which expression means **to accidentally tell a secret**?
    ☐ let the cat out of the bag.
    ☐ hit the nail on the head.

40. Is this sentence correct? ☐ yes ☐ no
    The herbivore devoured the grass, hay and leaves.

MY SCORE

1. Circle the correct spelling.   ambitious   ambicious

2. Circle the correct spelling.   ceiling   cieling

3. Add the silent letter.   dou___t

4. Circle the correct spelling.   noticeable   noticable

5. A synonym for *rot* is:
   ☐ rote   ☐ decay   ☐ decoy

6. *currant* or *current*? _____
   The river's .... is quite dangerous.

7. The contraction of **will not** is _____ .

8. Circle the correct homophone.
   The guessed/guest in Room 101 is very polite.

9. Circle the word with fewer syllables.   initial   special

10. Rewrite each word with *ing* added.
    write _____   begin _____

11. Add one comma.
    Arriving at the theatre Emma felt a knot in her stomach.

12. Enclose the additional information in commas.
    Emma was auditioning for a play her first one and she was very nervous.

13. Add a comma or commas to the sentence.
    Emma wondered which part she was best suited to: the sports fanatic the teacher or the cook.

14. Circle the pronoun.
    If you have a bacterial infection, the doctor may prescribe a course of antibiotics.

15. Circle the verb group.
    Antibiotics are produced by bacteria and fungi.

16. Circle the noun the pronoun refers to.
    Alexander Fleming noticed that when close to it, bacteria were killed by penicillin.

17. Write the missing pronoun.
    Although Fleming is famous for discovering penicillin,
    _____ *had first been noticed by a French medical student.*

18. The underlined word is a verb?   ☐ yes   ☐ no
    Some years later, two other scientists developed a medicine using penicillin.

19. Add the correct form of the verb **to cause**.
    Now, diseases and infections _____ by bacteria could be treated with penicillin.

20. Add the correct part of the verb **to be**.
    After penicillin became widely available, it was
    found that some bacteria _____ resistant to it.

21. Circle the correct spelling.   siege   seige

22. Circle the correct spelling.   protein   protien

23. Add the silent letter.   solem___

24. Circle the correct spelling.   adoreable   adorable

25. An antonym for **bright** is: ☐ brilliant   ☐ gloomy

26. Add the suffix **ant** to **serve**. _____

27. *roots* or *routes*? _____
    The capital city has a lot of .... into it.

28. Write a synonym for **buy**.   p_____

29. Listed alphabetically, the second word is _____ .
    flare   flimsy   flatter   flicker

30. Which word does not belong in the group?
    stem   soil   flower   leaf

31. Circle the speaker and the words spoken.
    The crowd screamed, 'We want Three Connections!'

32. Add punctuation.
    The pop group appeared on the balcony. Greetings everyone We are so happy to be here

33. Add punctuation.
    Barry Tiles took the microphone. We dedicate this tour to our dedicated fans

34. Circle and write the proper adjective. _____
    Archimedes was an ancient Greek scientist and philosopher.

35. Circle the conjunction.
    Archimedes discovered how many mechanical principles worked and he wrote formulae to explain them.

36. Circle the proper noun.
    Archimedes invented the pulley system and a system for raising water from a low level to a higher one.

37. Circle the word meaning **discoveries**.
    When his country was under attack from invaders, Archimedes' inventions were extremely valuable.

38. Circle the word that means **on fire**.
    A mirror system, used for intensifying the sun's rays, set enemy ships alight.

39. Circle the superlative adjective.
    But Archimedes is most famous for his displacement of water theory which he realised while getting into his bath.

40. Circle the conjunction.
    Archimedes was killed by a Roman soldier while he worked on his calculations.

MY SCORE

1. Circle the correct spelling.   reccomend   recommend

2. Circle the incorrect spelling.   enviroment   environment

3. Circle the incorrect spelling.   baeutiful   beautiful

4. Circle the correct spelling.   garrantee   guarantee

5. A synonym for *isolated* is:
   ☐ island   ☐ solitary   ☐ soluble

6. Circle the correct prefix for the verb.
   The guard did not know if he had <u>un/re</u> locked the door when he left.

7. Expand.   where've _____

8. Circle the correct homophone.
   Our teacher has no <u>patience/patients</u> with us.

9. Count the syllables.   evaporation ☐   frequently ☐

10. Write the simple present tense verb for *he*, *she* and *it*.
    marry _____   supply _____

11. Write a suitable conjunction.
    Learning a foreign language can be fun
    _____ *I enjoy acting out everyday situations.*

12. Add commas.
    During my trip I went to Tralee Killarney Kenmare Cobh and Waterford.

13. Which is needed? ☐ a comma   ☐ a full stop
    I want to travel as soon as I leave school ☐ *but my parents say I have to earn some money first.*

14. Write the verb. _____.
    Julius Caesar was a powerful leader in Ancient Rome.

15. Circle the proper noun.
    He had many ideas for improving the republic of Rome.

16. Circle and write the adjective. _____
    Julius Caesar was a successful army general.

17. Circle the nouns.
    The senate worried that Caesar wanted to be king.

18. Circle the pronouns.
    They were right to worry because Julius Caesar wanted to rule the republic himself.

19. Circle the two prepositions.
    Julius Caesar was assassinated by members of the senate.

20. Write the correct part of the verb *to become*.
    The nephew of Julius Caesar _____ *the first emperor of the Roman Empire.*

21. Circle the correct spelling.   convenience   convience

22. Circle the incorrect spelling.   forgiveible   forgivable

23. Circle the incorrect spelling.   discipline   disipline

24. Circle the correct spelling.   mischievous   mischievious

25. An antonym for *sensible* is:
    ☐ absurd   ☐ abstract   ☐ sensitive

26. Add the suffix *ise* to change the noun to a verb.
    memory _____   apology _____

27. *pair* or *pare* or *pear*? _____
    I love to eat an apple and a .... for dessert.

28. The word *summit* comes from the Latin word *summus* meaning: ☐ highest   ☐ middle

29. Listed alphabetically, the last word is _____.
    brush   browse   bruise   brute

30. Which word does not belong in the group?
    ash   water   lava   magma

31. Add commas.
    I read novels by authors such as Emily Rodda JK Rowling Rick Riordan and Suzanne Collins.

32. Circle the word that means a person who studies living things.
    geologist   astrologist   biologist

33. Add an apostrophe.
    The childrens books were all over the table.

34. Circle: ☐ present tense   ☐ past tense.
    For early explorers, a sea journey between the east and west coasts of the Americas was a very long voyage.

35. Circle the noun the pronoun *one* refers to.
    Whether they sailed north or south, the voyage to the opposite coast was a treacherous one.

36. The underlined word is a conjunction.   ☐ yes   ☐ no
    As a safe route to the north <u>was</u> not discovered until 1903, early ships had to traverse the wild seas around Cape Horn.

37. Circle the prepositions.
    The Panama Canal creates a short-cut, through Central America between the two oceans.

38. Circle the error.
    Construction took ten year to complete.

39. Circle the pronoun and the noun it refers to.
    Even though it runs through the country of Panama, the canal is an international waterway.

40. Circle the definite article.
    With queues and three sets of locks to navigate, it takes about 15 hours to complete the short trip.

MY SCORE

1. Circle the correct spelling. scedule schedule

2. Circle the incorrect spelling. feud fued

3. Circle the correct spelling. apolergise apologise

4. Circle the incorrect spelling. definite definate

5. A synonym for **durable** is:
   ☐ duress ☐ sturdy ☐ stupid

6. Circle the correct prefix for the verb.
   I <u>dis/un</u> like overripe bananas.

7. Expand.
   when're _____ when've _____

8. Circle the correct homophone.
   A <u>currant/current</u> is like a small raisin or sultana.

9. Count the syllables. experiment ☐ ecosystem ☐

10. Add the simple past tense for the third person singular.
    hurry _____ supply _____

11. Punctuate.
    show me your homework demanded the teacher

12. Punctuate.
    my favourite subjects are history geography and science

13. Punctuate.
    michael morpurgo wrote the book war horse

14. The sentence is in the _____ tense.
    Goree is an island just off the coast of Senegal, West Africa.

15. Circle the verb group.
    For three hundred years, the largest slave trading centre on the African coast was housed on Goree.

16. A ☐ preposition ☐ conjunction follows the verb group.
    The slaves were separated from their families.

17. Circle the word that connects the two sentences.
    A corridor led to 'the door of no return' and a jetty from which the human cargo was loaded.

18. Rewrite the sentence in the correct order.
    maltreated the slaves by were traders
    _____

19. Circle the preposition.
    Millions of people left their homeland in this terrible way.

20. Circle the phrase that refers to Goree Island.
    This island of shame stands as a memorial to the suffering endured by so many.

21. Circle the incorrect spelling. prejerdice prejudice

22. Circle the correct spelling. sausage sausidge

23. Circle the incorrect spelling. government goverment

24. Circle the correct spelling. consience conscience

25. An antonym for **adore** is:
    ☐ adorn ☐ detest ☐ detect

26. Add the suffix **ion** or **ation** to change the verb to a noun.
    erupt _____ preserve _____

27. **site** or **sight**? _____
    The workers on the building .... were exhausted.

28. Write an antonym for **solid**. l_____

29. Listed alphabetically, the third word is _____.
    finance fillet finale filter

30. Which word does not belong in the group?
    grizzly zebra panda polar

31. Punctuate.
    that famous ballet was called swan lake

32. Punctuate.
    i actually enjoyed it admitted mark.

33. Punctuate.
    Can we go and see it in Vienna asked mark.

34. Circle the reflexive pronoun.
    The cat curled itself into a ball and slept.

35. Circle the pair of conjunctions that work together.
    Not only is this cat loved but also it is very spoilt.

36. Circle the definite article.
    Misty, the family cat, can do many things.

37. Circle the word that connects.
    Misty extends her claws and pulls the flyscreen door open.

38. Circle the preposition.
    Misty doesn't like it when she is moved from a soft chair.

39. Rewrite the sentence in the correct order.
    Misty we vet to drove the
    _____

40. Circle the proper noun.
    Before we had Misty, we didn't realise how much we would love her.

MY SCORE

1. Circle the correct spelling.   rassberry   raspberry

2. Circle the incorrect spelling.   desend   descend

3. Circle the correct spelling.   forgivness   forgiveness

4. Circle the incorrect spelling.   asisstance   assistance

5. A synonym for **surprise** is:
   ☐ survive   ☐ starter   ☐ startle

6. Circle the correct prefix for the verb.
   The team had to dis/re play the match.

7. Contract.   should have _____

8. Circle the correct homophone.
   The old beach/beech tree was struck by lightning.

9. Count the syllables.   deciduous ☐   coniferous ☐

10. Write the past and present participles of the verb **decay**.
    was _____   is _____

11. Match the underlined words to their meaning.
    Ⓐ *Mum gave me a small-cake recipe.*
    Ⓑ *Mum gave me a small cake recipe.*
    ☐ The recipe for the cake was small.
    ☐ The recipe was for small cakes.

12. Add speech marks to show direct speech.
    These cakes are delicious! sighed Ali. Any more?

13. Punctuate.
    Whos going to clean up Alis mess asked Mum

14. Circle the definite article.
    Everyone recognises the Statue of Liberty.

15. Circle the masculine noun.
    The man did not know where it came from?

16. Circle the prepositions.
    The statue was a gift to the United States from the people of France.

17. Circle the conjunction.
    The Statue of Liberty was built in France before it was transported, in pieces, to New York.

18. Circle the proper adjective.
    The statue commemorates the American Declaration of Independence which occurred on 4 July 1776.

19. Circle the verb group.
    America had been fighting for independence from Great Britain.

20. Underline the opposite of **enemies**.
    France entered the war as allies of the Americans.

21. Circle the incorrect spelling.   descision   decision

22. Circle the correct spelling.   circumfrence   circumference

23. Circle the incorrect spelling.   recent   rescent

24. Circle the correct spelling.   drout   drought

25. An antonym for **collect** is:
    ☐ collide   ☐ disperse   ☐ displace

26. Change each verb to a noun ending in **ion**.
    extend _____   confuse _____

27. **pain** or **pane**? _____
    The .... of glass shattered into tiny pieces.

28. Write a synonym for **interior**.   i_____

29. Listed alphabetically, the first word is _____ .
    charade   charisma   charcoal   charity

30. Circle the two words that are part of the same word family.
    flour   flounce   floury

31. Add the apostrophe.
    Tanya and Belles holiday begins in three weeks.

32. Add an apostrophe.
    Tanyas and Belles suitcases were too heavy.

33. Add the **apostrophe(s)** and the **letter s** if needed.
    Tanya___ and Belle___ flight was delayed by the storm.

34. Circle the correct word .
    Who is (smaller, smallest), Tim or Tom?

35. Circle the adjectives.
    The berries were so sweet and delicious.

36. Circle the pronoun.
    I couldn't stop eating the basket of delicious fruit.

37. Circle the adjective intensifier.
    That night, I had a really bad stomach ache.

38. Circle the infinitive in the sentence.
    I am never going to eat so much fruit at once, ever again.

39. Circle the infinitive of the verb.
    We need to store the jam safely in pots and jars.

40. Circle the nouns with common genders.
    church   baby   relation   goose   guest

MY SCORE

1. Circle the correct spelling.   accident   accerdent

2. Circle the incorrect spelling.   difficulty   dificulty

3. Circle the correct spelling.   hopeful   hopful

4. Circle the incorrect spelling.   posionous   poisonous

5. A synonym for **referee** is:
   ☐ reformer   ☐ umbrage   ☐ umpire

6. Rearrange the letters to spell the opposite of **private**.
   lupbic _____

7. Write the singular.
   teeth _____   children _____

8. Circle the correct homophone.
   The farmer will sew/sow the seeds in spring.

9. Count the syllables.
   alternatively ☐   consequently ☐

10. Write the past and present participles of the verb **drag**.
    past _____   present _____

11. Add speech marks.
    After reading the survey results, the councillor spoke. An adventure park will be built!

12. Add commas as needed.
    The next day plans for the park were drawn up.

13. Punctuate.
    the children will be able to play on swings slides climbing frames and tennis courts

14. Circle the verb group.
    In war, nuclear weapons have been used twice.

15. Circle the word that means **destroyed**.
    The cities of Hiroshima and Nagasaki in Japan were decimated by atomic bombs.

16. Circle the word that connects the two sentences.
    The war in Europe had ended in May, but the war in the Pacific raged on.

17. Circle the pronoun and the noun it refers to.
    The United States government called for the Japanese to surrender but they ignored the request.

18. Circle the indefinite article.
    On 6 August, a bomb was dropped on Hiroshima and three days later another hit Nagasaki.

19. Circle the proper noun.
    Within a week, Japan surrendered.

20. Circle the proper adjective.
    The effects of the bombings on the Japanese people have lasted for many years.

21. Circle the incorrect spelling.   curculate   circulate

22. Circle the correct spelling.   grieve   greive

23. Circle the incorrect spelling.   resistible   resistable

24. Circle the correct spelling.   rumour   roumur

25. An antonym for **seldom** is:
    ☐ selfish   ☐ fractionally   ☐ frequently

26. Change each noun to an adjective ending in **ive**.
    corrosion _____   information _____

27. **check** or **cheque**? _____
    Can you please .... it is locked.

28. Write an antonym of **superior**.   i_____

29. Listed alphabetically, the last word is _____ .
    spanner   sparse   sparkle   spatula

30. Circle the word that does not belong in the word family.
    carnivorous   devour   voracious   voucher

31. Add the apostrophes.
    Britains and Germanys leaders in WW I were related.

32. Add an apostrophe.
    George and Wilhelms grandmother was Queen Victoria.

33. Add the **apostrophe(s)** and the **letter s** if needed.
    George___ father and Wilhelm___ mother were siblings.

34. The sentence is a: ☐ statement   ☐ command
         ☐ exclamation   ☐ question
    In legend, the North Island of New Zealand is the fish of Maui, the demi-god.

35. Circle the masculine noun.
    The South Island is Maui and his brothers' fishing boat.

36. Circle the proper nouns.
    Stewart Island, in the far south, is Maui's anchor.

37. Circle the word that connects the two sentences.
    The legend tells of young Maui who hid on his brothers' boat so he could go fishing with them.

38. Circle the pronouns.
    By the time he was discovered, it was too late.

39. Circle the correct expression.
    to give the cold shoulder   to take the cold shoulder

40. Circle the expression that means to be suspicious.
    to smell a mouse   to smell a rat

MY SCORE

1. Circle the correct spelling.   accurate   acurrate

2. Circle the incorrect spelling.   discipline   disipline

3. Circle the correct spelling.   magitian   magician

4. Circle the incorrect spelling.   argument   arguement

5. A synonym for **courage** is:
   ☐ courtesy   ☐ bravery   ☐ brawn

6. Use the prefixes **mal** and **mis** to make two new words.
   nutrition _____   fortune _____

7. Write the plural or singular of each word.
   stapler _____   cities _____

8. Circle the correct homophone.
   The weather vane/vein was pointing south.

9. Count the syllables.   estimate ☐   evaporate ☐

10. Write the adverb from the adjective **ready**.
    adverb _____

11. Add the apostrophes.
    Toms leg broke when he fell off his twin cousins trampoline.

12. Write the contraction after each underlined phrase.
    Tom did not _____ *want to cry but he could not* _____ *help it.*

13. Punctuate.
    My leg will be in plaster for a few weeks explained Tom

14. Circle the verb group.
    The Suez Canal in Egypt was opened in 1869.

15. Circle the prepositions.
    This opened up a route between the Red and the Mediterranean Seas and the Indian Ocean.

16. Circle the proper adjective.
    The 160-kilometre canal was built using forced Egyptian labour.

17. **its** or **it's**?
    It is estimated that 120 000 workers died during _____ ten-year construction.

18. How many proper nouns? ☐
    The canal was closed during the war between Israel and Syria, Jordan and Egypt.

19. Circle the conjunction.
    Although the war lasted for only six days, the canal remained closed for eight years.

20. The word **revolution** means:
    ☐ a rebellion.   ☐ a type of gun.

21. Circle the incorrect spelling.   defernitely   definitely

22. Circle the correct spelling.   hemisphere   hemersphere

23. Circle the incorrect spelling.   laboratory   labratory

24. Circle the correct spelling.   prievous   previous

25. An antonym for **divide** is:
    ☐ division   ☐ unite   ☐ unique

26. Write each word with the suffix **ial** or **ular**.
    muscle _____   palace _____

27. **tail** or **tale**? _____
    His excuse sounded like a long ....

28. Circle the correct word.
    The ball hit my chest and waste/waist.

29. Listed alphabetically, the second word is _____ .
    scamper   scalpel   scarcely   scavenger

30. Circle the word that does not belong in the word group.
    generous   generation   generosity   generously

31. Add the commas. How many are needed? ☐
    Tina said 'Shall I invite Anna Mira or Jade?'

32. Add the commas. How many are needed? ☐
    Tina had friends from school swimming dancing and gym.

33. This sentence is in the _____ tense.
    Tina enjoyed an active lifestyle.

34. Circle the verb.
    At the Montreal Olympics, a Romanian gymnast scored seven 'perfect 10s' in her routines.

35. Which word means **without a single mistake**.
    Nadia Comaneci delivered flawless performances on the uneven bars and on the beam.

36. Circle the word that connects the two sentences.
    The scoreboard did not show double figures so Nadia's score of 10.00 had to be shown as 1.00.

37. Circle the word that is not needed.
    No-one in Olympic history time had ever scored a perfect 10 in a gymnastic event.

38. Circle the infinitive.
    Nadia was to become famous because of her achievement.

39. Circle the word written once and **understood** twice.
    Nadia left the Montreal Olympics with three gold medals, one silver and one bronze.

40. Circle the error.
    In moscow four years later, Nadia Comaneci won two more Olympic gold medals.

MY SCORE

1. Circle the correct spelling.   parallel   parralel

2. Circle the incorrect spelling.   separately   seprately

3. Circle the correct spelling.   embbarrased   embarrassed

4. Circle the incorrect spelling.   assthma   asthma

5. A synonym for **sufficient** is:
☐ superfluous ☐ adequate ☐ adjacent

6. Use the prefixes **inter** and **trans** to make two new words.
action _____   section _____

7. Write the plural or singular of each word.
deer _____   formula _____

8. Circle the correct homophones.
Check/Cheque your wallet for the check/cheque.

9. Count the syllables.   fascinate ☐   glossary ☐

10. Write the adverb and noun from the adjective **disastrous**.
adverb _____   noun _____

11. Add capital letters where needed.
franco was a spanish dictator who ruled spain.

12. The dash shows: ☐ repetition   ☐ interruption
*'Life under Franco's rule was just—just terrible!'
remembered an old Spanish farmer.*

13. Punctuate.
*europe has seen many notorious dictators such as
hitler stalin and mussolini*

14. Punctuate.
Kevin asked what does 'notorious' mean

15. Circle the superlative adjective.
*Haiyan was one of the strongest tropical cyclones on
record.*

16. Circle the verb group.
*About 4000 people died as the island nation was
battered by this destructive force of nature.*

17. The sentence is in the _____ tense.
*About 11 million people in the Philippines were left
homeless by Typhoon Yolanda.*

18. Circle the word that means **help or aid**.
*In a country where the people get no government
assistance, many were left with nothing.*

19. Circle the verb.
The Philippines received support from around the globe.

20. Circle the adjective and its intensifier.
Organisations collected urgently needed supplies.

21. Circle the incorrect spelling.   burglar   burgler

22. Circle the correct spelling.   association   asociation

23. Circle the incorrect spelling.   reahersal   rehearsal

24. Circle the correct spelling.   suspiscion   suspicion

25. An antonym for **perfect** is:
☐ perform   ☐ flaunt   ☐ flawed

26. Add the suffix **ment** to give the noun.
engage _____   attach _____

27. **right** or **rite**? _____
I don't think that is ....

28. Write an antonym for the word **superior**.   i_____

29. Listed alphabetically, the first word is _____.
incense   incredible   incident   include

30. Circle the word that does not belong in the word group.
appear   appeal   appearance   appearing

31. Which adjective phrase needs a hyphen?
☐ *The holiday was much needed.*
☐ *The much needed holiday was enjoyable.*

32. Add a hyphen.
*By Tuesday afternoon, two fifths of the school week is
over.*

33. Add a hyphen.
In secondary school, classes last for thirty five minutes.

34. Circle the conjunctions.
*The cyclist conquered not only the world's toughest bike
race but also its deadliest disease.*

35. Circle the adjective.
The inspirational athlete never gave up.

36. Circle the common noun.
*Everyone was amazed by this athlete who had been so
close to death.*

37. Circle four prepositions.
*Many people benefited from the charity he established
for treatment of and research into the disease.*

38. Circle the word that means to improve.
*But some people believed the cyclist had used drugs to
enhance his performance.*

39. Circle the adverb.
He eventually admitted he had used drugs.

40. Circle the abstract noun.
His confession upset many people.

MY SCORE

1. Circle the correct spelling.   desperate   desparate

2. Circle the incorrect spelling.   acquisition   aquisition

3. Circle the correct spelling.   humilaty   humility

4. Circle the incorrect spelling.   repetition   repatition

5. A synonym for **synthetic** is:
   ☐ synchronised   ☐ artistic   ☐ artificial

6. Use the prefixes **sub** and **super** to make two new words.
   conscious _____   charge _____

7. Write the plural or singular of each word.
   fungus _____   pianos _____

8. Circle the correct homophones.
   I'm hoarse/horse from calling my hoarse/horse.

9. Count the syllables.   omnivorous ☐   nocturnal ☐

10. Write the adverb and noun from the adjective **certain**.
    adverb _____   noun _____

11. Punctuate the sentence.
    is it true that if you dont have a healthy diet your body will suffer in the future

12. Correct any punctuation errors.
    These days Dads favourite hobby is gardening.

13. Add a full stop (**.**) question (**?**) or exclamation (**!**) mark.
    Gardening can be relaxing ☐ *Have you tried it* ☐

14. Circle the three prepositions.
    During WW I, countries involved in the fighting used the services of a canine army.

15. Circle the verb group.
    There were many ranks in this army and dogs were trained to serve in a specific one.

16. Circle the infinitive verb.
    Sentry dogs were trained to react when an intruder approached a secure area.

17. Insert **its** or **it's**.
    On foot patrol, a scout dog would stiffen and point
    _____ *tail when it detected an unfamiliar scent.*

18. Circle the plural nouns.
    Casualty dogs, equipped with medical supplies were trained to find the wounded and dying.

19. Circle the prepositions.
    Communication between the trenches was carried out most efficiently by messenger dogs.

20. This sentence is in the _____ tense.
    Dogs were pets to the troops who needed them.

21. Circle the incorrect spelling.   enfusiasm   enthusiasm

22. Circle the correct spelling.   catastrophy   catastrophe

23. Circle the incorrect spelling.   polititian   politician

24. Circle the correct spelling.   patiance   patience

25. An antonym for **gentle** is:
    ☐ generous   ☐ ferocious   ☐ festive

26. Add the suffix **al** or **ous** to give the adjective.
    torture _____   culture _____

27. **their** or **they're** or **there**? _____
    That is .... car.

28. An antonym for **polite** is **i**_____.

29. Listed alphabetically, the second word is _____.
    galaxy   gallant   galleon   galore

30. Circle the word that does not belong in the word group.
    defence   deficient   defensive   defend

31. Add apostrophes as needed.
    Saturdays and Sundays weather was terrible.

32. How many meteorologists? ☐ one ☐ more than one
    Add the apostrophe.
    Many meteorologists predictions are accurate.

33. Rewrite the phrase with an apostrophe.
    the plans of the weekend
    _____

34. Circle the superlative adjective.
    Every year, Rio de Janeiro hosts the world's biggest carnival.

35. Circle the verb group.
    Rio has been holding festivals for almost two hundred years.

36. Circle the verb infinitive.
    About two million revellers crowd the streets each day to witness the amazing spectacle.

37. Circle the verb.
    Groups design floats for the carnival parade.

38. Circle the plural nouns.
    The singers and dancers must perform for the whole time while the floats are on parade.

39. Circle the adjective intensifier.
    Costumes are elaborate and can be extremely heavy.

40. Circle the nouns with common gender.
    The dancer and singer were exhausted at the end of the parade.

MY SCORE

1. Circle the correct spelling.   alturnately   alternately

2. Circle the incorrect spelling.   corossion   corrosion

3. Circle the correct spelling.   estury   estuary

4. Circle the incorrect spelling.   percieve   perceive

5. A synonym for **embarrass** is:
   ☐ embassy   ☐ humility   ☐ humiliate

6. Use the prefixes **post** and **pre** to make two new words.
   mature _____   script _____

7. Write the plural or singular of each word.
   radius _____   analyses _____

8. Circle the correct homophones.
   As winter war/wore on, the war/wore continued.

9. Count the syllables.   tragedy ☐   sediment ☐

10. Write the adverb and noun from the adjective **grateful**.
    adverb _____   noun _____

11. Add a comma or commas to the sentence.
    Before the arrival of the railways people did not stray very far from their home towns.

12. Correct any punctuation errors in the sentence.
    many people believed the railways would destroy the countryside.

13. Punctuate.
    The teacher explained The railways didnt destroy the countryside

14. Circle the proper nouns.
    Each summer, Pamplona in northern Spain is the venue for a crazy, possibly lethal festival.

15. Circle the word that means **a very large area of land**.
    A seven-day 'running of the bulls' festival is held in honour of the patron saint of the region.

16. Circle the conjunction and the phrases it connects.
    Human competitors run through the streets just ahead of six adult bulls and a few young steers.

17. Circle a word that means **viewers**.
    Spectators are kept safe behind barriers but hundreds of runners are injured each year.

18. ☐ An infinitive ☐ A preposition follows the verb group.
    The bulls are destined to die in the bullfight.

19. Write 14th in words. _____
    The festival tradition dates back to the 14th century.

20. Circle the conjunction.
    Runners wear a red bandana tied around the head or waist.

21. Circle the incorrect spelling. reclamation reclaimation

22. Circle the correct spelling.   optimism   optimmism

23. Circle the incorrect spelling.   desicive   decisive

24. Circle the correct spelling. consequently conseqently

25. An antonym for **abundant** is:
    ☐ abolition   ☐ measure   ☐ meagre

26. Add the suffix **cious** or **tious** to give the adjective.
    malice _____   nutrition _____

27. **permanent** or **temporary**? _____
    The .... pain will only last for a few seconds.

28. The word **stellar** comes from the Latin word **stella**
    meaning: ☐ shine   ☐ star

29. Listed alphabetically, the third word is _____.
    kindle   kitchen   kidnap   kiln

30. Circle the word that does not belong in the word group.
    object   oblige   objectively   objective

31. Add capital letters where needed.
    The Nile was very important to ancient egypt.

32. Insert the missing punctuation mark.
    When it flooded ☐ it left a layer of fertile soil.

33. Insert the missing punctuation mark.
    Did you know this fertile soil is called alluvium ☐

34. Circle the verb group.
    All living things have been classified into groups.

35. Circle the proper adjective and the verb infinitive.
    A Swedish scientist designed a way to classify living things.

36. Circle the pronoun.
    When new species were discovered, they could be classified by answering yes or no to a series of questions.

37. Insert an appropriate word.
    There were two main _____, plants and animals, which were then further divided.

38. Circle the plural nouns.
    Scientists have since agreed that there should be more groups, or kingdoms.

39. Insert an appropriate word.
    Some scientists work on _____ kingdoms of life: plants, animals, fungi, protista and monera.

40. **to** is: ☐ a preposition   ☐ part of infinitive
    Humans belong to the animal kingdom.

MY SCORE

THINGS I NEED TO REMEMBER